GENERATIONAL GLOW

Nurturing Spaciousness and Flow in Ourselves and Others

HEATHER SCHERF, MS, LPC

BALBOA.PRESS
A DIVISION OF HAY HOUSE

Balboa Press books may be ordered through booksellers or by contacting:

Balboa Press
A Division of Hay House
1663 Liberty Drive
Bloomington, IN 47403
www.balboapress.com
844-682-1282

ISBN: 979-8-7652-4914-7 (sc)
ISBN: 979-8-7652-4913-0 (e)

Library of Congress Control Number: 2024908517

Print information available on the last page.

Balboa Press rev. date: 05/17/2024

CONTENTS

INTRODUCTION

Generational Glow

One day, I was in deep meditation. I was listening to an audio-guided meditation by *Rising Higher Meditation* on YouTube (Sheppard 2023). In this specific meditation, the creator guided me through a visual journey on a yacht. While engaged in it, I could feel the energy of the visualization as if it were happening. I saw myself on the side of the yacht that was toward the beach. My toes were in the sand. I was playing with a jellyfish. The jellyfish was magnificent in all its luminous colors. I held it and played with it. It was not stinging or causing me any pain. I had not previously had an affinity for jellyfish, and I had never had any trauma associated with one. This is the reason I knew it was a message that would be significant to me.

Upon completion of the meditation, I looked up the spiritual meaning of the jellyfish. To my surprise, I found two main themes. The first was the jellyfish Christianity term, and the second was the flow, trust, and surrender term. At that time, both held meaning. I was questioning my own faith and spirituality, as well as trying to learn to reduce rigidity in my own mind and flow and to trust the universe. I had to unlearn everything I had learned in forty years of life and to rewire my entire being to reduce rigid debilitating thinking.

Here is a flow state definition:

> The state of being where it is not about control, nor outcome. But rather, about creation, flow, and ease. It is about being present in the moment. (Cziksentmihalyi 1990)

Jellyfish are amazing creatures. They have the natural ability to produce their own light in a process called bioluminescence. Two molecules—luciferin and luciferase—react with oxygen and produce their radiant and vibrant colors. Luminescence means to glow, shine, and/or radiate light (National Geographic, 2023). Jellyfish tend to just flow through the waters in a fluid way with absolutely nothing on their minds. Well, it's because they do not have brains. However, what a nice thought: to flow without thought but only light—no thoughts but just vibes. Jellyfish live alone sometimes. However, most of the time, they tend to be found in groups called shoals and swarms. Extremely large groups of them are known as blooms (Bioexpedition 2023).

As we already know, light itself cannot be created or destroyed. And darkness is simply the absence of light. We know that we can affect the darkness by turning a flashlight or a lamp on. But did you know that humans can radiate light also? A study from 2009 by Japanese researchers found that bioluminescent light exists in humans; it's just too dim for our human eyes to pick up. Furthermore, our metabolic rates have an impact on our light (Hryla 2016). Things that affect our metabolic rates are activities that use the most energy. This study indicated that there are times of the day when we glow the brightest, such as early afternoon in the peak of the day.

We also already know that oxytocin or the love hormone affects us so much when we are in love that it gives us a glowing effect. Oxytocin, dopamine, and serotonin boost our abilities to trust others, have human connections, feel empathy, and bond with one another (Dictionary. com 2023). When we love, we glow. When we fear, we dim.

Light itself is defined as one type of radiant energy (Solar Schools 2023). Emotion is defined as energy in motion. If it is not expressed, it is repressed, which is another way of saying that we as humans have the tendency to block our own light. Emotions are the experience of energy moving through the body. Emotional energy will try anything it can to be released from our bodies. When we find ways to block it, we end up storing it in our cells. We learn to bypass our emotions by dissociating, having addictions, experiencing perfectionism, and judging ourselves and others (Gill 2023).

With all that said, we as humans absolutely can radiate our own light. We can take our fears and transmute them into love and light. Transmuting means to change the form of something (*Merriam-Webster Dictionary* 2023).

Mental alchemy is the process of using your mental capacity to change yourself and your circumstances, in form, appearance, or nature (*Merriam-Webster Dictionary* 2023). Spiritual alchemy is the process of freeing your spiritual self from your fears, limiting belief systems, and lack of self-acceptance. The word *alchemy* on its own is the art of transformation, inner liberation, and change (*Merriam-Webster Dictionary* 2023).

In this book, I aim to support you in the process of your own alchemy from your fears or darkness so that you can allow your light to radiate with yourself and others. Each of the fifteen chapters will guide you through the process of transmuting fear into love. And if you do that, you can glow like the jellyfish. If we all do that as individuals within family dynamics, we can bloom together.

Humans are malleable, in flux, ever-changing, and fluid. Our natural desire is to not be rigid but instead to be flowing. Our resistance to it as a society keeps us stuck in so much pain. When we lean into flow for ourselves, we feel lighter, more joyful, and less tense.

This introduction section will briefly review four key areas that are relevant to the book's entire mission. First, we will examine a brief overview of societal expectations and the fears we all have as humans. Second, I will give you a few definitions and distinctions surrounding the ego versus the spirit or soul, duality versus non-duality, and religion versus spiritualism, for context of the book's organization. Third, we will take a brief look at what generationalism is and how to remember our sameness and humanness. Fourth, you will look at your specific family lineage and some things to consider so that you can find compassion for one another's generation. This introduction's intention is to set the framework for understanding why the book is structured into fifteen fears, as our fears come from all these different spaces: our society, spirituality, religion, faith, generational differences, and unique family lineage.

Societal Fears and Expectations

Our American society places a lot of conditions and expectations on us. Society expects us to overwork, succeed, and produce. That is how our success as humans seems to be measured. This culture supports the breeding of these fears, and this can manifest as mental health symptoms such as anxiety and depression. Examples of some of these fears are below.

- We are alone, different, and separate from one another in our lives.
- Time is limited, and it should be rushed.
- People should never leave us.
- If we aren't 100 percent whole, we are not aligned with ourselves. We are all broken if we are not whole.
- We don't learn from our relationships.
- Love is an act and not a state of being. We shouldn't want higher love and should accept people as they are.
- People who hurt us do not deserve our compassion.
- People who hurt us do not deserve our forgiveness.
- People must agree with us and have the same values and beliefs in life if we are to feel connected.
- Emotional intimacy expects perfection.
- Our purpose in life is to work our lives away. As adults, we aren't allowed to play. We must always produce.
- We are only allowed to be good at one thing. We must be experts in one profession.
- Our physical bodies must always be healthy, fit, lean, and aesthetically perfect.
- We must always know the outcome to something; otherwise, there is no purpose in doing it.
- We must always be able to make decisions; otherwise, something is wrong with us.

Our mind likes to buy into these fears as our stories. Our internal wars become our external battles.

Below are fifteen beliefs that promote spaciousness, flow, and peace instead of fear. They are points of peace that can keep us feeling more in a state of flow within ourselves. They also can be thought of as choices, acceptances, rights, or remembrances. These fifteen are the structure of the book's chapters.

The Fifteen Fluid Points of Peace

1. We are never alone, and we are always connected.
2. Time is not linear, and there is no rush.
3. People never leave us; they just shift timelines.
4. We are always whole, in alignment, and not broken.
5. Discernment is a lifelong work of art.
6. Our relationships are our teachers.
7. Love is a state of being; it is who we are.
8. Our ability to have compassion for another is endless, yet we get to decide whom we give our compassion to. (Compassion is a spectrum.)
9. Our ability to forgive another is endless, yet we get to decide whom or if we forgive. (Forgiveness is a spectrum.)
10. Our individual perceptions are vast and unlimited. (Perception is a spectrum.)
11. Emotional intimacy is not perfect, and it doesn't expect perfection.
12. Our primary purpose in life is to experience love, joy, play, and all the spectrum of human emotion.
13. We are all multi-passionate and multitalented beings.
14. Our bodies are just vessels for our spirits or souls.
15. Letting go of an outcome frees our souls to flow.

In this book, we will look at our individual fears and where they came from. We will look at remembering who we really are when the fear is stripped away. We will explore how this relates to your family interactions and learn ways to discuss this together.

Ego versus Spirit, Duality, and Faith

Here are some important definitions retrieved from the *Merriam-Webster Dictionary*.

Ego: the self especially as contrasted with another self or the world

Duality: the quality or state of having two different or opposite parts or elements

Mindfulness: the practice of maintaining a nonjudgmental state of heightened or complete awareness of one's thoughts, emotions, or experiences on a moment-to-moment basis

Dichotomous: dividing into two parts

Generational Glow isn't meant to be a finite book, such as *Ten Key Ways to Detach from the Mind* or *Ten Ways to Live Your Best Life*. It is meant to show and illuminate that everything is *limitless*. I want to show you the beauty of the spectrum of fluidity.

As humans, we like organization, structure, bullet-pointed lists, planners, and the like. They are all useful constructs that the human mind made to be able to function in our society. But our spirit knows there are infinite amounts of possibilities in life, love, and the choices or decisions we make. The ego fights with this daily through the mind's system of dichotomous thinking. It wants to fit everything into a box with a lid and to move on.

Reducing dichotomous thinking allows you to hold so much space for love, compassion, and grace. It doesn't mean perfect, but it does mean that compassion and empathy lead me in how I make decisions and relate to others and the world around me.

But when we get out of the rigidity of the mind and into the spirit, the spirit knows more than the mind. It knows without being taught. There is an inner knowing that exists without the feelings and thoughts associated with dichotomous thinking. It helps remove all unneeded fear-based judgment.

Black and white thinking is another way of saying dichotomous thoughts. Consider some all-or-nothing, good-versus-bad types of thoughts that you tend to think of. Examples of this include, *I didn't get the position at work, so I must not be good enough. That person never texted me back, so that individual must not like me.* Because we tend to think this way, we often make conditional statements about ourselves. What are some conditional statements you say about yourself? Examples include, *If I don't get that job, I am not worthy. If that person doesn't want to date me, I am not good enough. If I don't produce this project, I am not good enough.* What are some unconditionally loving statements you already say to yourself?

This book will be using words like *spirit, soul, God, consciousness,* and *faith.* I want to make a very important distinction here. The following summarizations were retrieved from the National Center for Cultural Competence. Religion is "a set of organized beliefs, practices, and systems that most often relate to the belief and worship of a controlling force, such as a personal god or another supernatural being." Spirituality is "an individual's search for ultimate or sacred meaning, and purpose in life. Additionally, it can mean to seek out or search for personal growth, religious experience, beliefs in a supernatural realm or afterlife, or to make sense of one's own inner dimension" (National Center for Cultural Competence 2023).

According to some estimates, four thousand religions, faith groups, and denominations exist in the world today (CNBC 2023). The soul is "the immaterial essence, animating principle, or actuating cause of an individual life, and/or the spiritual principle embodied in human beings, all rational and spiritual beings, or the universe" (*Merriam-Webster Dictionary* 2023). Consciousness is "the state of being awake and aware of one's surroundings, Or the awareness or perception of something by a person" (*Merriam-Webster Dictionary 2023).*

There is a lot of confusion out there about religion versus spirituality. Religion is a set of values and beliefs that humans have. Spirituality is the process by which we search for our beliefs. I am not telling you what to believe about your own religion, faith, spirituality. I am simply trying to guide and bring conscious awareness to what your beliefs are, how you got there, how they help, and how or if they hurt. I am not proposing that following a religion or spirituality means that one is better or worse than another. I am not sticking up for one more than another. I am simply talking about the science behind transmuting our fears into love and emotions into energy.

And yes, I will use these words in my own flowing manner throughout this book, as I enjoy writing about it. It does not mean that you have to take it with you if it does not connect to you due to a religion or spiritual belief system that you follow. I am just here to support in bringing conscious awareness to fear and love—period.

From Generationalism to Sameness and Oneness

I am a therapist by trade. One of my passions is observing or noticing the differences across generations. It's interesting to go back to the idea that as humans, we all want the same things. We want to love and be loved, but we have different methods of getting there.

I work with children, teens, adults, couples, and families of all ages and stages of development. Thus, I get to see their development over a life span and those generational differences every week at my job. I love talking to every client from each generation and hearing his or her worldview, perspective, and wisdom. Each generation has wisdom to offer. Because of that, my job is never boring.

In my first book, *Apples and Avalanches: An Exploration for Caring for the Severely Mentally Ill* (2022), I wrote about generational differences and touched on the topics within this book. This book is an expansion of the first one, in that I will specifically try to give tips and tools for talking with family members across generations.

For a quick reference, Statistica labels the generations as the following:

Silent Generation: born between 1928–1945

Baby Boomer: born between 1946–1964

Generation X: born between 1965–1980

Millennials: born between 1981–1996

Gen Z: born between 1997–2012

Generation Alpha: born between 2013–2023 (Statistica 2023)

When the silent generation, boomers, or generation X come to therapy, they talk about things such as work, productivity, retirement, and aging in American society. When Millennials or younger generations come in, they talk about self-care, boundaries, mental health, and parenting troubles. They long for jobs and positions that promote balance and wellness. They talk about soul-searching and finding themselves.

When millennials or younger generations come into the therapy office, they talk about the pressures to work and succeed by society's standards. This ranges from the overachiever to the underachiever, who wants to defy society's expectations around work over wellness. The other generations discuss this as well, but then it is a generalized idea.

Yet there are commonalities in being human. All are talking about their relationships to some capacity. All long to connect with the generation before or after them.

We are currently living in a time of chaos and major change in our society. Traditionalists and boomers never heard of the phrase *coping skills* prior to this decade. They didn't even know it was a thing. They also never focused on words such as *self-regulation*, *self-awareness*, and *healing journey*. The shift of caring about mental health started during younger generations. Thus, now in therapy, the boomer and older generation are unpacking all of that.

Middle-aged individuals and younger generations had the luck to be there while that was shifting, and they know what mental health and self-care are. They had opportunities at a younger age to get in touch with their inner beings through therapy and self-help. So millennials and younger generations, this is a call to action for you—to have compassion for the older generations. Imagine growing up in a time where you just went to work, worked hard, and went home.

Vice versa, the flipside of this is that younger generations are growing up in chaotic times. They have never known what it's like to play outside until the lights come on and feel safe or to attend school without worrying about guns and violence. You are the generations that value language that is more neutral, positive, and nonjudgmental. You value self-care over work and balance over productivity. Yet you are growing up in an age where attending college is still a societal expectation or norm. You are taking AP classes, doing two-to-four after-school sports and activities, and because of that, you never sleep while in high school or college. Dear generations that did not attend college, please have empathy for this. Literally, they don't sleep these days in high school and college.

But millennials and younger generations also spend a lot of time on media, which unfortunately has both its positives and negatives, right? A negative would be how much external validation we seek through social media to feel relevant. And I hate that for you. This is from a caring therapist.

But there is also a push to not work as much. And in my opinion, this is rightfully so. It's one of the wisest things of your generation—to work less, make the most money you can, and have balance in personal life. Bravo! No one wants to work his or her life away. At the heart of every generation, people truly don't want to work that much. But boomers and older generations didn't have that choice, so obviously, there is some resentment there. Really, it's jealousy, and that is OK. If I was a boomer, I would be jealous too. It's a useful emotion. If you are a boomer or from an older generation who is reading this book, do you feel jealous of that? I don't mean this in an offensive way. It just depends on our values.

My point is that these are the things generations fight about: values surrounding work, money, productivity, retirement, human rights, reducing shame in culture, LGBTQA+ rights, female reproductive rights, and the list continues. As we all know, these topics can present in our own families in different ways.

We struggle to have conversations because these are emotionally triggering topics for so many of us. We can't talk about the big topics like the ones above. To talk about other things as well creates distance. If we don't feel comfortable having conversations about what is going on in our world and lives, why talk? We all end up sitting together or even in separate rooms, playing on our phones or mindlessly scrolling to self-regulate after working or going to school and doing activities all day or night. We are exhausted, so we disengage. It's just easier to keep moving on the hamster wheel of our busy schedules and find twenty minutes of nothingness or cat videos on TikTok. Most of the time we either don't talk about things at all or say too much to one another, which comes across as super judgmental or ill intended. It causes arguments or families to break up.

Remember, we are living in a time where four generations have very different ideas about how to talk about feelings. Elder generations never talk about feelings, and the younger ones talk about them all the time. Thus, it doesn't matter if we are talking about a big-ticket item like human rights or simpler things in our daily lives, such as homework and studying. The values are all different across generations.

So what is similar across generations? For starters, the fact that everything mentioned above makes most of us feel unheard, alone, unseen, lonely, isolated, depressed, anxious, overworked, and underpaid. That is all of us. We all feel a variety of these emotions. And all generations want to love and be loved. All generations want to live a good life and die. All generations want to feel like they left a mark on the world and their families, careers, and friends.

We must remember who we are at our cores. The problem isn't one another. The problem is the problem. The problem is that we don't know how to talk—period. That is no one's fault. It is not one generation's fault.

Plenty of families out there do have conversations that are meaningful, about difficult subjects, and where all parties are respected and valued. I don't know them because I am a therapist.

People only tend to come to therapy when something is wrong. So I want to give kudos to those individuals and families who already do it well.

The goal and intention of this workbook is to help bridge conscious connections across generations. I want to see three-to-four generations sitting at a dinner table and having calm, collected conversations about the smaller things and the bigger things. I want them to feel more connected in the process. I want to see people shift toward living in a space of compassion and nonjudgment for themselves and their connections because it's a beautiful thing. We all want this; we just don't know how to get there. The internal war within us about our beliefs regarding generations also becomes an external war.

Besides generational differences, we have different paces at which we learn and experience things. Developmental psychology focuses on certain tasks humans should be able to do by a certain age, as well as certain phases we go through across a lifetime relative to our age (American Psychological Association 2014). These developmental or milestone differences are standard for psychology. However, if we also step outside the box of psychology, we can see that we all learn at different rates and paces. What we are supposed to learn at age thirty, we sometimes don't learn until we are fifty. If we attach too much meaning to things we are supposed to do by a certain age, we end up shaming ourselves and others who don't live to that standard.

One simple example is a thirty-five-year-old woman coming into the therapy office, who is upset because she has yet to get married or have children. Because of society's belief systems, and the structures of human psychology, she may feel a lot of shame that she hasn't met this milestone yet.

A second example would be a twenty-five-year-old male in the therapy office who has shame because he never went to college or had any education post high school. Now he is stuck in depressive cycles, thinking he did something wrong because he did not choose to go to college at all or by a certain time frame.

In what ways did you age-shame yourself in this manner? Have you ever done this? If you answer no to this question, I would be immensely surprised. Humanity has a way of putting people in boxes and timelines that just aren't true. There is no one way or right way to do life at any capacity.

There are studies that research the effectiveness and usefulness of the myths of generationalism. These studies indicate that trying to research such large groups of people and placing them in categories are not helpful or useful. Human beings are too multifaceted to be categorized (Rudolph 2020).

Think about this. Have you ever felt like you fit in your generation's stereotypical belief systems 100 percent of the time? During the time you have been on this earth, have you always followed what is perceived as normal or typical phases or milestones of life you should achieve by age X? Also, have you ever met anyone else who meets either the criteria of always believing what a certain generation believes or falling in the perfect milestone-phase-of-life timeline? I have never met either of those criteria. I have never 100 percent believed or even identified myself as a millennial. I haven't perfectly matched some psychologist's viewpoint or definition of what normal life phases should be.

To be clear, I am not saying these structures of thinking are bad. They are useful in contexts where they are just that—useful. I look at them this way: If by looking at generational or developmental milestones helps you have empathy for others or understanding for myself and others in some way, then yes, they are useful and helpful. However, it becomes non-useful if it starts a judgment or shaming cycle on yourself or another. If it invites a war, it is not useful. If it invites a reason to play the blame or shame game, it is not useful. When we use it against one another, it has detrimental effects on our connections and our own self-worth.

I have never met anyone who was OK with being measured this way, have you? Yet we are all guilty of measuring ourselves and others in this way, even on a subconscious level and when we don't mean to. It's so engrained in us. We are conditioned as humans to believe in generational and developmental boxes. If we don't fit in those boxes, something is wrong with us. Thus, I am inviting you to reflect on, consider, and assess your own relationship with these concepts. Ask yourself if they are helpful or harmful to hold onto.

As a side bar message, I once was reading about reincarnation. Those who believe in reincarnation believe the soul keeps cycling through the heavens and back into a body on Earth. If this is true, does age even exist? If our soul can reincarnate lifetime after lifetime, how do we know whose soul is older or younger? This gives us something to think about in terms of age-shaming behaviors or belief systems. How do you know your grandparent's soul is older than your soul? It's food for thought.

In summary, the proposal of this book wants you to consider throwing out the window ideas related to generational differences and stereotypes for the sake of saving yourself from shaming your experience as a human. Throw them out the window for the sake of saving your relationships with loved ones. If you must keep them, use them only for empathy and understanding and not bashing or blaming.

We are fluid beings, in flux, malleable, and always evolving and changing. I propose that instead of looking at others and our differences, we look at finding sameness and points of peace within our stories and pain.

Our minds like to create narratives based on our lives' experiences and the emotions related to them. We all tend to want to be the hero of our own story. We all attach to stories of resilience, triumph, hope, perseverance, passion, forgiveness, love, healing, and change. Some stories are of being the victim, vigilante, or villain. Our stories can be based on our traumas and very deep pains. It is the way our minds make sense of our experiences and the world around us. These stories keep us protected like a veil of safety. It's just something we do as humans.

Yet with the fears we have from societal expectations and our traumas, generational differences, and developmental milestone differences, we wrap all of that into our unique story. Yet the irony is that we all have a story. Just because our story is different, it does not mean the pain underneath is not the same.

People today are fascinated with exploring their own traumas. Everywhere we look, we are inundated with trauma, as individuals and in our families, cultures, politics, and beyond. Our desire to be heard right now is very loud while our desire to hear others can, at times, be low. It feels like our society is trying to balance out. All are screaming to be heard and seen, but as we scream louder, another person softens his or her voice. It can feel like we are collectively on this generational quest for authenticity. We all want to live authentically and to have meaningful connections.

However, sometimes we can become too attached to our own stories or to our traumas. Remember that thought comes from the mind. The essence of who you really are is your spirit. With that said, we are not our traumas. We are not broken. We are not all victims. If we attach too much to our trauma, we get stuck in cycles of pain. Everyone has trauma. Your story deserves a safe space where people are willing to hear it and at the pace you want to share it. And yes, some trauma is so unimaginable that it can be very hard and take a long time to unravel in therapy.

However, the point I am trying to make here is that sometimes because we have traumas, we have stories. We sometimes forget that others do too. We sometimes forget that even though our story isn't the same, the pain underneath is valid for us all. Our internal battles become our external wars.

I would like to propose something. While reading this book, notice the stories you have about your life experiences and consider another person's story. Look for points of sameness in the pain of the stories. You will learn to see yourself as you really are and not what society thinks you should be and to see others as they really are. We are not different from one another just because our stories are different. They are what make us the same.

Also, examine the stories we have not yet traveled. Ask yourself while looking at your own life timeline what stories you have created for your future based on your desires and hopes. What stories have you created based on defeat and fear? Notice it without judging yourself.

If we are at war with someone else, we have a war within ourselves longing to be resolved. Look at your stories and internal wars. Don't rush to resolve and judge them, but rather, bring awareness to them. If you are willing to find fluidity within yourself, your connections will flow easier as well. Internal fluidity=external fluidity. This book is an invitation to remember who we all really are—fluid and malleable beings.

Finding Compassion in Family Lineage

Taking it a step further, investigate your own family's history and generational patterns. Ask yourself the following question: Was I emotionally safe?

Did you feel safe with your time and how you used it within your family? Or did you feel rushed?

Did you feel you were allowed to be creative with your time, or did you feel restricted by it?

Did you feel safe and permitted to make decisions and choices?

Did you feel safe to change, or were you worried and fearful of judgment from family members?

Did you feel you were allowed to not be OK and to not have all the answers to your life at any given moment? Were you allowed to feel broken?

Did you feel you were allowed to grieve changes and the loss of loved ones or friends, or did someone around you make you feel you weren't allowed to have thoughts and feelings regarding those changes?

Did you feel safe to learn as you went across this lifetime? Or were you expected to have it all together?

Did you feel safe to choose who you were going to love romantically? Or did you feel that no matter who you chose, it would be judged? Did other people try to tell you what love was or was not by their own definition, or did they let you learn on your own?

When you showed love, compassion, or forgiveness to others who hurt you, did you feel safe enough to do that? Or did you feel judged and bogged down by your family's influence?

Did you feel safe to talk about different feelings, opinions, and ideas with family members? Or was it mostly was met with judgment or resistance every time you did this?

During your imperfections, did you feel safe to be loved unconditionally?

Did you feel safe to explore what purpose means to you? Did you think you had to have it all figured out or your family would judge you?

Did you feel safe to play, create, express, and build? Or were you told that play and expression are only for children?

What about your physical body? Did you feel safe to have a different aesthetic than the people in your family?

Did you feel safe to explore your faith, spirituality, religion, and other belief systems around life, or did you fear it would be met with ridicule and judgment?

Did you feel safe to be loved, deserve love, and love others?

Were your parents and the ones whom you held close to your heart safe?

Now that you have asked yourself these questions, ask your parents, grandparents, great-grandparents, and ancestors. Run though the above questions and be curious about their histories of feeling safe in their family lineage. I don't think they ever felt fully safe in all these ways. Have you ever met anyone who felt safe in all these ways? I haven't. In family lines, sometimes it's easy to see the generational patterns around feeling safe and sometimes not so much. For example, if on one side of your family you see a lot of anxiety and ambivalence around change, there is most likely a history of anxiety around change in your family line.

All this is to say that you shouldn't take generationalism at face value. Get curious about the specific differences and patterns in your family around time, change, love, purpose, forgiveness, passion, play, faith, spirituality, and more. Not every family fits in the typical generational stereotypes' box. We know that generationalism helps us remember wars, chaos, the Great Depression, 9/11, and every change on a societal, cultural, and political level. Yet to summarize our own family lines and to say, "Oh, it's just their generation," is a non-inclusive and minimizing look at the individual people within the family.

We need to try to look at one another with curiosity, tenderness, softness, spaciousness, and vastness. We need to stop speaking and instead focus on seeing, observing, and listening while remembering our sameness and vastness—oneness rather than separateness. Not feeling safe from generation upon generation isn't an excuse for bad behavior. Yet they make us aware. They are a way to find compassion in our family lines. They are being brought to light to transmute and heal our connections.

These generational patterns can be seen as curses, loops we get stuck in, history repeating itself, and cycling through. What generational loops or cycles are your family stuck in? What does your family already do well, in terms of providing emotional, physical, mental, and spiritual safety? Your family may be able to do half of the chapters in this book well. If so, acknowledge and appreciate those and hold space for the success as well. How did we succeed at allowing space for X, Y, or Z within one another?

Everywhere we turn, there are judgments, opinions, traumas, and fears. They take up a large amount of space. But if we are willing to see the alternative of vastness, openness, spaciousness, and limitlessness of ourselves as human beings, a new world of opportunity for connecting with loved ones awaits. It is one that is not finite, doesn't have an end or beginning, but flows in the space together of infinite possibilities.

We don't have to hold so tightly to all this anymore. Within our family lines, we are allowed to release the burdens of chains, loops, and cycles. We get to choose whether or not to meet in a safe space. We get to choose to meet one another there. Let's meet one another there.

Structure of the Book

The structure of the workbook is as follows. Part 1 of the book is called "Individual Flow." You will take a deep dive into your own inner being through the fifteen internal wars in the workbook. The fifteen sections were made to use individually. It gives you a chance to look within and learn before trying to converse as a family. You may find that not all fifteen are something you want to talk about with a family member, partner, or friend. But all fifteen will benefit you as an individual.

I recommend that the fifteen chapters be done at a pace that feels comfortable to you. They are easy and quick reads, as they are only a few pages each. You may choose to do one a day or a couple per week. There is no right or wrong way to complete it. You just don't want to rush the book. Sometimes when we allow space between chapters while reading a book, it gives us time to think.

Part 2 of the book is called "Family Flow." After you have gone through the fifteen individual sections, you will be ready to do the activities and discussions together as a family. The "Family Flow" section specifically guides you in ways to communicate around the main categories and themes of the book. It will give you some questions to explore together. The key in this section is to apply what you learned from the previous sections so that you can have conscious conversations.

By the end of this book,

1. I hope that you learn to implement non duality and compassion in your individual life so that you can feel freer and more peaceful in general.

2. I hope that the fifteen points of peace help remind you who you really are—heart and spirit rather than the mind and ego.
3. I hope this book gives you courage to be the authentic person you really are.
4. I hope this book helps pull out of you the beauty and awesomeness that already exist within you and that your ego's mind patterns slowly fade away.
5. I hope this book helps open your heart to love, romantically and platonically. Maybe the gates and doors you kept closed will open.

As a family, couple, or friend—whoever you are reading this book with—I hope you collectively

1. Learn to have conversations that are based in wanting to learn about one another and from a space of curiosity instead of needing to control.
2. Sit at the same dinner table and have conversations about various topics without wanting to flick broccoli at one another.
3. Learn to agree to disagree with one another and accept one another for the person he or she is at this moment in time and moving forward.
4. That we can learn to encourage one another being more consciously aware of our language (without placing unneeded expectations on one another)
5. Look at one another as equals and reduce the power dynamics in your connections. It's time to let go of the notion that older equals wiser. It does not help your conversations. Instead, see one another for who you really are.
6. Look at one another and see what is already good.

And when you have completed this book, I hope you continue to remember what you learned about yourself through the process as your life moves on. I hope you read more on the topic of flow state for individuals, conscious partnerships for couples, and mindfulness from Eckhart Tolle and others. This workbook is a creation of a therapist, who loves all of this and various theories. It is just an introduction to what you could learn about at the start of the desire you have for conscious connections.

With all of this said, I want to notate a very important disclaimer. You cannot expect that after reading this book, you will be able to live perfectly and consciously aware 100 percent of the time. That is not the message I want readers to receive. I don't want anyone thinking, *If I don't use this stuff 100 percent of the time, I am failing.* No. Conscious awareness itself is flowing. There will be moments in your life when you will be more consciously aware at a rate of say 80 percent or higher. There will also be moments when you will only be able to be consciously aware 50 percent or less of the time. The progress we make with anything in life is not linear or permanent. That is part of one of the fifteen internal wars as well.

Also, please be advised that this stuff is *hard*. Acceptance of the fact that this stuff is hard takes the pressure off. We are literally trying to train our hearts and spirits to lead, instead of our minds and egos. That is no easy feat. Telling our minds to take a back seat is our hardest work!

Thus, if you get discouraged or frustrated for a moment, pause and praise yourself. The fact that you are here is amazing. The feelings of discouragement or frustration will pass, as all feelings are only temporary. Just sit with it for a moment, notice it without judgment, and watch it float away on a balloon into the ether. Stay with me on this journey. You are not alone.

In conclusion to our introduction section, I hope you learn a lot of stuff. I hope you flow with your new fluid flexes. It's rad if you do. Oh wait, is rad a cool word anymore? Oh, I know. I hope you slay it. I hope you understand the assignment and share tea with your friends. Let's learn to change our vibes, get rid of the sus energy, and re-vibe to groovy love. OK, I will see myself out.

There's one more thing. On YouTube, watch the scene from the Adam Sandler and Drew Barrymore movie *Blended* (2014) where the character is singing, "We are blending."

We're blending, we're blending, we're blending when anotha comes togetha.

You're welcome. Now you have that song in your head.

Let's get started. Let's navigate that beautiful heart of yours. Are you ready to examine your fears and to free them so that you can remember who you are? Are you ready to get to know your heart? I am excited for you. Let's do this. Drop out of fear and into love.

Do you remember the Celine Dion song from *Beauty and the Beast* called "How Does a Moment Last Forever"? (2017) It's such a beautiful song. I cry every time. The song goes

How does a moment last forever?

How can a story never die?

It is love we must hold on to

Never easy but we try.

Seriously, though, that song causes you to feel. Am I right? If I could pick any song that matches what I am trying to express in this book, this would be one of the main ones.

Setting Intentions

What do you hope to shift, change, modify, or learn about yourself as you go through this workbook? Use the section below to create some goals for your experience with this book. For example, do you hope that by the end of it, you learn to change the way you forgive others? Do you hope to have more freedom from your mind? Do you want to learn about your family patterns? Do you want to learn how to communicate with others better?

My personal intentions and goals for this book are as follows:

1. _____
_____
_____
_____

2. _____
_____
_____
_____

3. _____
_____
_____
_____

4. _____
_____
_____
_____

5. _____
_____
_____
_____

Throughout this book, I want you to notice your feelings. Notice the somatic feelings and sensations that come up for you when reading different sections or words. Do you have sensations such as a temperature change, butterflies in your stomach, nausea, lightness in the body, playfulness, love, heaviness, fidgetiness, or others? If you do, pause and just notice it. I want you to feel the energy of your emotions and thoughts while not judging them as good or bad.

Notice if anything excites or inspires you and follow your intuition to note that in the book. If something inspires an idea for you, it is your love energy sneaking through and speaking to you. Honor and notice that. If you like one of my ideas, build on it and create. We are all cocreators here.

PART 1
Individual Flow

CHAPTER 1

The Fear of Feeling Alone

Potential assumptions and fears say, *I am alone, and no one understands me.* Spaciousness and flow say, *We are all connected, interdependent, and never alone. I am never alone, even if I'm sitting physically alone. We are all connected and similar beings. There are helpers everywhere. There are also people we have yet to meet. You are not alone in your story. I am never alone, and you are never alone.*

Before-Reading Reflection

- What is my current relationship like to the idea above?
- What are my current beliefs about the idea above?
- Out of those beliefs or values, which of them already help me?
- Out of those beliefs or values, which of them hurt or keep me suffering in some way?
- What people, places, and organizations (spiritual, religious, educational, political, or other) have contributed to my current belief systems?
- What did my family of origin believe regarding this idea?
- What is something I wish would happen regarding this idea and in relation to how I live my life?
- Do I notice any dichotomous (all or nothing) thinking patterns regarding the idea above, which keep me suffering?
- Do I notice any conditional statements I make regarding the idea above?
- Do I notice any pressures I put on myself regarding the idea above?

We are all connected as humans and interdependent on one another for both survival and love. It is easy to forget this as humans. If we are physically sitting alone and spending a lot of time with our own presence, we can feel emotionally alone and isolated. It can feel like no one cares.

When talking about mental health and depression, if we buy too much into thinking we are alone, it can fuel those symptoms. It can be hard to hold onto being interconnected. Yet we have all had periods of loneliness. And the process of that in life is fluid as well. Sometimes we feel more connected to others, and sometimes we feel lonelier.

Let's talk about the differences between three different words that have the word *dependent* in them: *codependent*, *independent*, and *interdependent*. Depending on your own understanding, history, and relationship with those three words, thinking of them may illicit a different emotion or thought process within you. For example, the word *codependent* can have a negative connotation in our society. If you are *codependent*, it implies that you overly rely on others for emotional, spiritual, financial, and physical support of some kind. For example, you overly rely or depend on others to validate you in some way. You may ask others for help paying your bills or providing another form of physical support such as housing. Maybe we overly rely on other people's opinions and feedback because it's hard to discern our own and make decisions. And yes, there is truth to this word. But sometimes we get fixated on thinking we are codependent to the extent that we view reliance on other people as a bad thing.

This brings us to the word *independent*. We think, *Oh, crap, I am codependent. I'd better change that. I want healthy relationships. I want to be able to stand on my own two feet before I can be in a healthy romantic relationship.* And just like that, we have placed a conditional statement on something that didn't need a condition. Read that again. You do not necessarily have to be fully independent before you are lovable or worthy of love. So then we go down this path of thinking, *I have to fix myself in every way. I need to be productive, have my own finances, and not rely on anyone else, emotionally, physically, or otherwise. I must be strong. Stand on my own two feet. Be indestructible.* But if we go too far that way, then what happens? If we seek our own independence, what do we lose out on? The answer is our general connection with and need for others. And in some ways, if we are independent for too long, it becomes a way for us to keep our hearts locked up. We think, *If I don't need anyone, and I can completely take care of myself, why do I want or need to connect with others? I can now even love myself. What do I need anyone for? I love me. I am healed and fixed!* This may sound dramatic but follow me here. Sometimes, we can take that too far and forget that we are interconnected and interdependent beings.

Merriam-Webster Dictionary defines *interdependence* as "the dependence of two or more people or things on each other" (2023). *Independence* is "a condition where someone or some institution or some other entity is capable of existing on its own without having to rely on others to sustain itself." *Codependence* is "excessive emotional or psychological reliance on a partner." So while we see definitions and labels as good versus bad, and while I am joking about the independent person's need to feel whole on his or her own, it is easy to look at this and also see a process of change. Instead of thinking, *I am codependent, and that is bad*, think, *I have some behaviors and needs that I overly rely on others for. Maybe it's worth looking at. But I am not broken. It is not bad. It is just a pattern that I need to engage in at some point in my life to get some type of need met. That is all.* But even if we would consider ourselves to be more codependent at certain times in our lives, it means that at that time, we still valued our connections and saw them as needed, helpful, and useful. We still knew that we needed one another and that we were connected, even in our codependency.

The search for independence and the phase of learning about your own independence are useful and necessary. The seasons of singleness we experience, for example, have endless lessons, which give us confidence to stand on our own two feet. Our independent season teaches us what we want and don't want in life, what our hearts desire, what we're willing to accept or not accept, and more. Ironically, we do come back from that space desiring more connection with others. We realize how interdependent and connected we are. A helpful reframe is seeing these three words as phases of a giant process or cycle. We will have phases of needing others at different rates depending on where we are in our lives.

When you are feeling alone, ask yourself, *Am I really alone, or out of fear they would not understand, am I not talking to the people or helpers around me who are available?* There are people around you who will remind you how loved, valued, and needed you are. If you are single or just feeling alone, maybe this part of your journey is about learning how to love yourself and manage your own emotions alone. Maybe this period of aloneness or singleness is just a growth period.

And so we come to interdependence. We can still rely on others if we are standing alone. You are not alone, even if you're physically spending a lot of time alone. There are people around you who love and support you. Here is a little guided meditation about the way that feeling alone is related to time:

> While on the Bridge: A Reminder You Are Not Alone. A Reflection of Memories.
>
> If we look at our memories and look around ourselves currently, we will see we are not alone.

When fear about time steps in, it says, *Hurry! You're late. You're getting old. You're too slow; go faster.* When your spirit steps in, it says, *You aren't late. You are right on time. Slow down and trust the divine timing of your life.*

It's the quality of our moments in life that tether to us our heartstrings. Or is it the quantity of moments that matters more? Think about your own relationship with time. Ask yourself what the top-ten moments of your life have been. Why are they the top-ten moments? My first thoughts are of skydiving, traveling to Mexico, camping, going to Grandma's house in my pajamas and getting snacks, and sharing powdered-sugar donuts with my pap. Sure, all those are great. But what about the time in between those moments? What about the moments of pain, sadness, loneliness, and confusion? Did they also matter? Could some of our more painful moments be as meaningful? These moments feel more like a collection across time; all are equal in value and add to the enrichment of our lives and souls.

Fights with family members are some of the most influential moments because after we fight, we release and build anew. We stitch one another's hearts back up and move on. And there is the moment (or several) of reflection, right after the pain but before the next moment of glory (whatever that is for you). Pretend you are sitting on a bridge in that moment, feeling alone. When you stand on the bridge and look back, you see everyone you have ever loved and every experience behind you. Every person or pet is there like a giant family selfie. You can feel the love and pain simultaneously, yet the memory of the love is the brightest. It's a giant photo montage of your life. Who and what do you notice the most? Who are the influential souls you have met, encountered, lived with, and grown up with? What were the more influential moments for you?

Then you look forward from the bridge and at the grass. Instead of a giant photo collection of all the moments, you see five different portals. The portals radiate with different colors but emanate various possibilities of your life, all of which you get to choose. Who or what do you see in those five different portals?

There are moments in your life when you are on the bridge, hanging out, unsure, fearful, and hopeful. Underneath the bridge is a healing body of water. The river is flowing freely. While you are on that bridge, oscillating between looking back at the collective moments and the future of what's in the portals, your human mind questions everything and anything. Your ego does not like the unknowns, so it will try to fill in the missing pieces with assumptions and fears. But if you take a moment to just sit on the bridge and notice what is around you, you see that there's a space right there that is beautiful—the now and present moment.

Using all your senses, what do you experience? Do you hear the water currents hitting the rocks? Do you see your feet dangling off the side of the bridge and underneath it, the sun hitting the water and the green land all around? The bridge is a rustic color, and it has ivy growing up a pillar. Small flowers grow from the ruins and rocks on the side of the river. There are squirrels in the trees, and birds are singing.

Do you feel gratitude? Do you feel peace? Do you feel your heart saying thank you to all the collection of moments in the past and the life you have not yet lived? Do you feel compassion for yourself and others? When you run across that bridge, you don't feel that as much. Sit there and allow your imagination to run wild. Down the river, an endless number of others are on bridges, simultaneously experiencing life at different rates and points across their own bridges. They are a bunch of beautiful souls on their own bridges, trying to figure out their next steps. Yet it's at these moments you allow yourself to sit on the bridge and just *be* and notice.

This thing called life is difficult. But you'll notice you're never truly alone. When you look back and see your past—loved ones and everyone who has ever been part of your life—you look forward to the portals and keep your mind open to the different possibilities ahead of you. People are there too. You have yet to meet these people. You have yet to have these experiences. Just because your mind can't figure out what's ahead doesn't mean what lies ahead is bad.

You look to the left or the right and see everyone is on a bridge. You look up and see the divine. You can see that all the bridges look like the collective consciousness. We are all here in this thing called life, and we are always connected. Envision further that the bridges are all connected in the sky like a giant spider web but also a pretty rainbow web of energy. The web is led by God.

So when you are on the bridge or in a moment of transition in your life, and your ego is saying, *I am late. I better hurry. I feel alone. I am getting old*, or other variations of pain, just take a seat right there, be, and notice, without any judgment on yourself or your feelings. You are not late, early, or behind; you are right on time with the divine.

Don't run across the bridge. Don't try to crawl under it, climb up it, scale the sides of it, or try to take any other alternate route. Your mind will try to do that during moments of pain and transition. It says, *Nope! I am not hanging out there and feeling my feelings. No thank you!* Just lightly stroll and sit. What we resist persists. Just allow it and flow. And if you're ever lonely, look right, left, or up. You can always ask your neighborhood friend on the other bridge if he or she can come sit with you on your bridge for a while.

On my bridge, I have a coffeemaker, Dunkin Donuts coffee, and varieties of flavored creamer. I am a great sharer. If you have the donuts, I'll bring the coffee. And even if you don't have donuts, I will still share.

Our interdependence can be seen across time and space. We are all connected, learning, from one another, and growing.

After-Reading Reflection

- Was there anything from this section that resonated with me and that I would like to start using or practicing in my life?
- Is there anything from this section I would like to slightly modify to fit my way of thinking or believing and my value system, to move forward in my life? (Remember that you are here to explore and create your own values.)
- Is there anything from this reading that brought up something I would like to talk to a loved one or family member about?
- Based on my values related to this topic, what are my boundaries around this regarding other people? And what will I do when someone does not respect my boundaries around this idea?
- Moving forward, how will I discern what is healthy versus not healthy for me in regard to this idea?
- Moving forward, my new relationship with this idea or philosophy is_____.

CHAPTER 2

The Fear of Time

Potential assumptions and fears say, *My time always feels rushed. There is not enough time. I feel like I am wasting time. My time on Earth is limited, so I need to hurry. I feel I am overworking during my time. I am aging quickly.* Spaciousness and flow say, "The ego is impatient because it knows its time is limited. The spirit is patient because it knows it is eternal" (Anonymous Author). *I have a right to slow down and not rush. I have a right to be fluid with my time and discern what I want to do with it, without others' feedback or commentaries. I have a right to slow down to engage in relaxation and methods of self-care. Time is not linear, and there is no rush. I can do things at the pace I want and what feels good for me rather than what society expects from me.*

Before-Reading Reflection

- What is my current relationship like with the idea of _____ above?
- What are my current beliefs about the idea above?
- Out of those beliefs or values, which of them already helps me?
- Out of those beliefs or values, which of them hurts or keeps me suffering in some way?
- What people, places, organizations (spiritual, religious, educational, political, or other) have contributed to my current belief systems?
- What did my family of origin believe regarding this idea?
- What is something I wish for regarding this idea, in relation to how I live my life?
- Do I notice any dichotomous (all or nothing) thinking patterns regarding the idea above that keep me suffering?
- Do I notice any conditional statements I make regarding the idea above?
- Do I notice any pressures I put on myself regarding the idea above?

One thing we can all relate to is our struggle with time. We all have fears around not having enough time. Have you ever met another human who did not, on some level, worry about having enough time? Regardless of our developmental ages or generational differences, there is for certain some sameness within this story or the internal war on time.

Let's look at the fear of not enough time. A five-year-old says, "I don't have enough time to play." A high schooler says, "I don't have enough time to sleep because of my academics and activities after school." A thirty-year-old says, "I don't have any time to breathe because all I do is work and take care of children." A sixty-year-old says, "I am three quarters out of here, so what do I want to accomplish before I die?" An eighty-year-old says, "I wish everyone spent more time with me."

At the root of enough time is the societal conditioning of busyness and being rushed. We all have schedules packed to the brim with work, children's activities, chores, family and friend activities, workouts, and other commitments. We don't often have time to breathe. We don't often make time to breathe.

Let's look at the fear of doing enough with our time. Five-year-olds don't even question this yet. They just live in the moment and in play and creativity. That is how they know they are living their best lives. They don't yet have a clue what time is. Yet anyone from the age of learning developmental tasks to being able to discern and understand what the concept of time is through old age and death questions *Am I doing enough with my time?*

The sameness in this story is that at every age, from middle school onward, we are measuring our worth of time. *Am I doing enough for my family with my time? Am I doing enough with my career with the time I have? Am I spending enough time with my family?*

At the root of whether or not we are doing enough with our time is the societal condition or expectation that our worth is measured by what we do with our time. Is what we do enough? Who measures the "enoughness"? It is not you or me; it is the structure of our society placing us on hamster wheels of comparisons to others and what they do with their time.

All the fears about time ironically stem from our desire to love. We want to do everything we can with the time we have on Earth. We want to experience love and joy in a variety of ways. We want to spend enough time with our families and friends. We want to have a joyful and successful career. We want to play and have adventures and new experiences.

It's like we are all handed a marble of time at birth. Yet it is a marble; it doesn't have a clear end or beginning because it is in a circular sphere. We know that while we are all given and gifted time, we don't know how much time that is. We hold that marble of time in our hands, trying to guess and predict how much time we have here. We never have that answer until that time comes. Thus at times, we grieve time existentially and subconsciously. We fear loss of time in a variety of contexts. We all have certain beliefs surrounding what justifies a good life and how we should spend it. These fears make us have certain behaviors or thought patterns that cycle around time.

Something that can help get our fears out, which is related to time, is the following quote.

> The Ego is impatient because it knows it's time is limited. The Spirit is patient because it knows it's time is eternal (Anonymous Author).

7

Depending on what your spiritual and religious beliefs are, you may or may not believe that you have a spirit and that the spirit lives on after death. For any atheist-identifying friends reading this book, this part may not connect with you, and that is OK. If you don't have a belief in an afterlife of some kind, it can be even harder to connect with time and relate to it.

Yet regardless of spirituality or faith, we all can see and agree that from the perception of our minds, time is limited. One of the hardest things to reckon with is the idea that time will end for us. Yet our minds covet, barter, and fear time and losses related to it. When this happens, and the fears are intense, it is because we have stepped out of the present time.

For centuries, leaders in mindfulness have educated us on the impact of the present moment. Every mindful leader will say that when we step out of the present moment, we live in fear and that when we live in the present moment, we find peace. Relating to time and being in the present moment are two of life's most challenging battles of the mind. It is an ongoing, fluid, malleable, and in-flux goal across a life span. It is one that takes daily effort.

Yet if we reframe this to get out of our minds and into our spirits, we feel peace. Our spirits are eternal. They don't covet time because they know that time is all there is. They don't barter time because they have faith in endless time. They don't fear time, as they know time isn't linear but rather everlasting and beyond our human form. They don't fear the loss of others in the same way our minds do, as they know connection never dies. Thus, it is normal to fear and grieve time. We all do. Yet if we tap into the present moment, regardless of what is going on around our external world of busyness and being rushed, we feel more at ease regarding our relationship with time.

The idea of needing to be rushed, do, or be are an illusion. It is based on fear and is related to our societal structure around expectations of what is normal regarding time. Nothing has ever been falser. It is the idea that we do not have sovereignty in the way we live and spend our time. The one thing that keeps us stuck is comparing ourselves to others. Ask yourself the questions in the pre- and post-reading sections about your relationship with time. Really explore where your relationship with time comes from. Ask yourself how you want to relate to it while moving forward, regardless of what others say about your time or any hidden expectations about what others think you should do with your time. Allow yourself to be fluid in your own relationship with time so that it can bend and flow in the way you feel works best for you.

In terms of how time plays out in family connections, there is a lot to say. We all have hidden fears, values, and belief systems with time. Thus, we show these fears outwardly to people around us. We can accidentally or purposely rush others around time. We can accidentally or purposely place expectations on others about time, which damages our connections. If in any connection, we both become self-aware of how to relate to time, we can improve our connections. If we allow each other to be fluid with our time, we will argue less.

One thing we all know to be true is that while we are here, we have this beautiful gift of sharing time and space together and opportunity to exist at the same time. Try not to allow the mind's patterns around time to take away from that present moment. And when we start to allow our fears to shape our marble of time, we lose time. When we allow time to exist as is, it is clear and peaceful. Be fluid with your time.

After-Reading Reflection

- Was there anything from this section that resonated with me and that I would like to start using and practicing in my life?
- Moving forward in my life, is there anything from this section that I would like to slightly modify to fit my way of thinking and believing and my value system? (Remember that you are here to explore and create your own values.)
- Was there anything from this reading that brought up an issue that I would like to talk to a loved one or family member about?
- Based on my values related to this topic, what are my boundaries around this regarding other people? And what will I do when someone does not respect my boundaries around this idea?
- Moving forward, how will I discern what is healthy versus not healthy for me in regard to this idea?
- Moving forward, my new relationship with the idea or philosophy is_____.

CHAPTER 3

The Fears Related to Change in Our Relationships

Potential assumptions and fears say, *When relationships change or end, I won't make it through. If people don't choose me, something is wrong with me. If people don't choose me, something is wrong with them. People are not allowed to leave.* Spaciousness and flow say, *Connection never truly dies; it just shifts and jumps timelines. People never leave us; they just move on to something else. People are allowed to leave. I am allowed to leave. Relationships are allowed to change and be fluid.*

Before-Reading Reflection

- What is my current relationship like with the idea of changes in relationships?
- What are my current beliefs about changes in relationships?
- Out of those beliefs or values, which of them already help me?
- Out of those beliefs or values, which of them hurt me or keep me suffering in some way?
- How do I allow myself space to feel and grieve loss or change in connection?
- What people, places, organizations (spiritual, religious, educational, political, or other) have contributed to my current belief systems about changes in relationships?
- What did my family of origin believe regarding this idea?
- What is something I wish for regarding this idea in relationship to how I live my life?
- Do I notice any dichotomous (all or nothing) thinking patterns regarding the idea above, which keep me suffering?
- Do I notice any conditional statements I make regarding the idea above?
- Do I notice any pressures I put on myself regarding the idea above?

Connection never truly dies; it just shifts and jumps timelines. Our ego minds don't like change in general. Thus when it comes to any type of relationship or connection changing, the ego will try to fill in the unknowns or create narratives. Our minds may say things like, *Screw that person. If they don't want to be in my life, forget them and others like them.* Our minds are just trying to make sense of the pain we feel emotionally and viscerally.

A helpful reframe is to view changes in relationships as people jumping timelines. We all have our own unique timeline in this life, with things, people, and places to experience. We are all living on our own timelines. But then someday, we meet at a crossroads on our timelines for a couple of months, a few years, or a decade. And sometimes we leave each other's timelines. It's not that the other person abandoned or left your timeline. It's more that we both naturally resumed or redirected our own timelines. And that is OK. The ego wants to fight these changes. Maybe the simple answer is that we are at different places in our learning, growth, and development, which doesn't support each other physically being in each other's lives at this time.

Yet sometimes separation is a teacher. Separation can sometimes be the most loving response to each other's growth processes. It allows spaciousness for it to grow or us to grow as individuals. Sometimes that person tends to show up back in our lives, which means we both just did another timeline jump. The connection never truly dies or ends; it just changes form, intensity, and frequency. Once we have that bond to someone, it doesn't just end. All connections have energetic cords tied to them—a story, thought, feeling, or memory. Energy itself doesn't change. This is true of romantic and platonic connections.

Our minds and hearts will say, *I don't want to lose that person. I don't want my life to change because that person is not physically in my life.* And of course, it is OK to be sad about these changes. Our consciousness says what is meant for us will never pass us by. If it is meant for us at this time in our lives, it will be here. If it is meant to come back, it will. Maybe the connection needs a pause.

But if we take that pause, break, or temporary disconnection, it doesn't mean that we aren't still energetically connected in our hearts in some way. It is now just a different way. Maybe we are still energetically connected by the beautiful memories we shared or one singular impactful moment we had with that person. Certain songs bring back those memories. Those moments of memories stay with us in our hearts and souls for eternity. Thoughts, memories, and feelings are all forms of energy. Thus, we hold them in our hearts with love and gratitude. And then we embrace what's next on our timelines without fear. We trust ourselves more with that perspective. We release the fear and control surrounding it with that perspective. We free ourselves from our own suffering with this perspective.

Did you ever notice the pattern of people bobbing and weaving out of your life? That is jumping timelines. Do you have friends whom you don't see or talk to for years, but you pick up where you left off? What about ex-romantic partners or long-lost family members? Our egos label this as negative. Our consciousness and spirits know there is a higher meaning to why people enter, exit, and potentially reenter our lives.

What I love to ponder is all the possibilities in that. The unknowns become less fearful and more playful and curious. I think, *Hmm, I wonder if that person will ever pop back up again in this lifetime?* Almost as if I am playing an energetic game of Guess Who? when that person pops back up. There's a sort of mystery in the unknown of that if you allow it. Sometimes it's nice to be surprised. How hard would it be to just let people go and release the fear of letting others go? We could notice it without the judgment of good or bad; it just is. How hard would it be to let people live on their own timelines with their own sovereign, unique choices and see what happens in the game of life?

And if they do not cross your timeline again, that doesn't mean it was for nothing. It just means that the person wanted something different at that time of his or her life. It isn't personal. It could be such a variety of reasons—developmental life circumstances, having children, working full-time, caring for a loved one, wanting a different life experience right now, or being focused on other things. We are so quick to personalize this. And personalizing it hurts us.

There may be some very solid and good reasons why someone having not been in your life is merited. But I am speaking about the people you are grieving the absence of. These are the ones you cry over when no one is watching and the ones you weren't ready to see leave. We hold onto memories, the lessons, and the visuals of what we thought that connection might look like over time. Maybe we envisioned growing old with that person. But here is a helpful question: What did any of that teach you? What type of lesson is there for you?

This doesn't mean that we overly attach unhealthy meanings to people that hurt us. It means that we allow things that we cannot control to just happen. We allow ourselves to feel frustrated and sad and then see or notice if there was a meaning to the experience for us.

When it comes to death, dying, and the grieving process, across religious and spiritual contexts, there is the belief that while they are gone, we are always connected. We are allowed to grieve the loss and change. Just because we cannot visually see a person in our reality, it does not mean that the energetic connection or bond is no longer present. Imagine if you allowed yourself to lean into this idea and belief. Maybe you already do.

I'm sure the harder the heartburn is, the harder it is to apply it to the situation. I'm talking about the person who broke your heart in the worst ways, the friend who betrayed you, and the coworker who talked about you. The higher the intensity, the harder it is to apply. But when you can use this idea, how relieving it is to allow people to be who they are and to make their own choices without control or judgment. To have this perspective is not to close your heart up and wrap it in a blanket of fear. Just notice changes in relationships with curiosity, compassion, and nonjudgment—and do it in your own timing and pacing.

And should we meet again on a timeline together, I'll look at you with compassion, an open heart, and curiosity instead of judgment. The space of time we spent apart I can almost guarantee taught us something! Later in the book, we will be looking at potential lessons or meanings behind our relationships and connections.

After-Reading Reflection

- Was there anything from this section that resonated with me and that I would like to start using and practicing in my life?
- Was there anyone I thought of while reading this who made an impact on me (a person I know longer connect with or feel distance from)? If so, what were the lessons I learned (if any) during that separation from them?
- What fears do I have regarding accepting the idea of jumping timelines?
- Moving forward in my life, is there anything from this section I would like to slightly modify to fit my way of thinking and believing or my value system? (Remember that you are here to explore and create your own values.)
- Is there anything from this reading that brought up something I would like to talk to a loved one or family member about?
- Based on my values related to this topic, what are my boundaries around this regarding other people? And what will I do when someone does not respect my boundaries around this idea?
- Moving forward, how will I discern what is healthy versus not healthy for me regarding this idea?
- My new relationship with change in relationships is_____.

CHAPTER 4

The Fear of Needing to Be Whole or Changing within Ourselves

Potential assumptions and fears say, *Change is scary. I won't survive this change. I can't have periods of life where I do not have everything together.* Spaciousness and flow say, *We are always 100 percent whole. We are not broken. We are always in alignment as we go on this journey called life. Our paths are unique to us. Everything is always changing and mostly for our learning and growth. I am allowed to be fluid in my learning process across my life span.*

Before-Reading Reflection

- What is my current relationship like with change in general?
- What is my current relationship like with the concept of learning and growth?
- What fears do I have about change, learning, and growth?
- What are my current beliefs about change?
- Out of those beliefs or values, which of them already help me?
- Out of those beliefs or values, which of them hurt me or keep me suffering in some way?
- What people, places, or organizations (spiritual, religious, educational, political, or other) have contributed to my current belief systems around change?
- What did my family of origin believe regarding change, learning, and growth?
- What is something I wish for regarding this idea, in relationship to how I live my life?
- Do I notice any dichotomous (all or nothing) thinking patterns regarding change, learning, and growth that keep me suffering?
- Do I notice any conditional statements I make regarding the idea above?
- Do I notice any pressures I put on myself regarding the idea above?
- How have I rushed myself to meet goals and change and pressured or shamed myself to meet those goals or aspirations in the past?
- Do I make any statements that compare myself to others in regard to change, learning, and growth? If so, how has that hindered my process or helped it?

If we accept that everything is always changing, our ambivalence to change decreases in intensity. If we accept that change is occurring constantly for our learning and growth, we gain wisdom. Nothing ever stays the same for long. How many times did those changes you experienced cripple your anxiety? What types of changes tend to trigger your nervous system more than others? Is it when you encounter a job, relationship, financial, or family change?

Also, what types of changes do you get through well? It's important to ask yourself this as well to be more strength based. Celebrate the types of changes you have gotten through because if you are roughly middle-aged and reading this book, you have gotten through many developmental life changes alone, let alone circumstantial ones unique to your life.

This chapter is twofold, as it takes a quick look at your relationship with change in general and your relationship to the concept of learning and growth. The words *alignment, wholeness,* and *healing* can have both positive intentions and negative connotations. Sometimes in movies and on TV shows, we see these characters who look like they have it all figured out. We see someone standing on top of a great big mountain with a beautiful physique. That person is smiling and looking like he or she has all the answers to life. That individual must be whole and aligned because he or she looks that way. And you think, *I want to be like that. Have life figured out and have all the answers.* It's this view of finality or a pinnacle presented in the movies. In this one moment, the individual is fully aligned, healed, whole, and poof that everything is fixed and that he or she will never have troubles again.

But the truth is that alignment is happening constantly within the presence of every moment. Not yesterday, not tomorrow, not until something is completed, but now. How can we have that moment on the mountaintop without walks in the valleys by the river down over the hill?

Alignment and wholeness can sometimes be perceived as you are not worthy until you are healed, or you must be good, or you are not whole; you are broken. It implies that we are somehow offtrack and not on course. We are always whole and where we are because we are supposed to be there. You may feel fragmented at times. But you are still whole.

A helpful reframe for yourself is the following: *I am just as aligned with myself now as I was five minutes ago, five years ago, ten years ago, and in this very minute. Whether I was hunched over in the fetal position crying over a deep pain, going through something terrible, or standing on top of the mountain, I was and am in alignment 100 percent of my life.* This reframe is needed in so many contexts. Our obsession with doing things, wellness, healing, etc., is a constant what we are doing right now isn't good enough vibe. We always want more. There is nothing wrong with goals, dreams, and wanting. Yet if it is constantly tied to our worth as human beings, where does that leave us?

Accepting where we are on our timeline is the key. If you feel disenfranchised, broken, unhealed, or whatever words you use to describe that, challenge that idea right now. Once for myself, I visualized my healing and personal growth and development as a simple baseball field. First base was my emotional well-being. Second base was my spiritual well-being. Third base was my physical well-being. Home plate was when I put all of them together and lived happily ever after. Poof! With one game of baseball, I was healed and magically put together.

A helpful metaphor to reframe this too is the following. Think of the baseball metaphor more as spiritual set points. We will most likely play roughly twenty-to-thirty baseball games in a life span of eighty-plus years on Earth. I'm just taking a wild guess here. The spiritual set points refer to the idea that right now, we are learning one lesson as we take the bases on the ball field and work through that particular lesson. When we round home plate, the lesson is learned—mostly. It may come up again in some other way in the future. But then we move on to another game of baseball to learn a new life lesson.

The pause between games is necessary too. Self-care and breaks help you assess how far you've come and cause you to reconsider some plays of life you want to change before the next ball game. So when you go on to game two or twenty-seven, you have fresh eyes. It is our active recovery in the game called life. We don't want to take the pain of the last game into the next.

It's important not to judge any part of the baseball game from a space of bad or good but to judge from a space of observation and noticing. If you want to hang out in the recovery period longer than that, it is OK too. There is no rush. Sometimes the energy of our goals, hearts desires, and feelings are so high and intense that we get excited about something and feel the need to hurry and rush. That is based on our society and perceptions around time. *I have to learn, or I am not as good. I have to do, or I am not as good.*

Life tends to teach us over and over again. When we rush or push, something gives, or it backfires. If we rush love, it runs. If we rush friendships or family members, they pull away. If we rush through pain, it follows us. If we rush to figure out our purpose quickly, we get met with more resistance.

And this is where my favorite meditation of the jellyfish comes in and reminds me to trust and surrender to the timing, flow, and process of my life. Relax, release control, follow your intuition, and surrender. I hope this quick metaphor helped. To view every experience you've had is useful in the very unique development of who you are. There are no other yous on this planet. You have experienced every piece of pain and disenfranchised part of you for a reason. Every part of love you have experienced was meant to show you something.

A second metaphor is a bridge and rainbow portal. We start on the bridge when we are all born in certain developmental phases. We then have opportunities to walk through new portals. Envision an octagon-shaped rainbow portal right now. Through that portal is a new level. We go through that portal and enjoy a period that feels peaceful and serene. The energy of that portal starts to fade, and then we step onto the next bridge.

The bridge is the time we reflect, ask questions, and learn new lessons. Each person is on the bridge for his or her own unique amount of time. Each person is walking through the next portal at his or her own unique time. But one thing is for certain; there will always be cycles, bridges, and portals. It doesn't end, meaning that change never ends. All of life is one big energetic ball of change—every thought, development, and connection.

What would be the point of life if we didn't have these cycles of change? What the heck would we be doing down on Earth? Would we all just stare at one another or walk around aimlessly? We wouldn't know anything that we know now if it had not been for change and evolution.

If we accept and visualize our life as bridges and portals, we see opportunity, fear change less, and learn to appreciate change more. Change can be seen as good if we slow down to observe and notice the progression. And if we can't see it as good, we can at least look at it from a more neutral space, which keeps us out of suffering.

After-Reading Reflection

- Was there anything from this section that resonated with me and that I would like to start using and practicing in my life?
- Moving forward in my life, is there anything from this section that I would like to slightly modify to fit my way of thinking and believing and my value system? (Remember that you are here to explore and create your own values.)
- How many cycles of big change have I been through in my life?
- How many mini changes have I been through in my life?
- After I experienced a cycle of change, was there relief or growth for me shortly after it in some way?
- Did anything I read bring up something that I would like to talk to a loved one or family member about?
- Based on my values related to this topic, what are my boundaries around this regarding other people? And what will I do when someone does not respect my boundaries around this idea?
- Moving forward, how will I discern what is healthy versus not healthy for me in regard to my relationship with change, learning, and growth?
- Moving forward, my new relationship with change is_____.

CHAPTER 5

The War on Discernment and Making Choices

Potential fears and assumptions say, *I fear making the wrong choices. I must always know what to do.* Spaciousness and flow say, *Discernment is a lifelong learning process and work of art. I am allowed to learn how to discern what is right for me at any stage of development. I am allowed to learn and grow throughout this life span. I am allowed to not have all the answers at any given time. I am allowed to learn something and reassess my desires, wants, and needs endlessly in this life.*

Before-Reading Reflection

- What is my current relationship with the way I make choices?
- What are my current beliefs about how I make choices or how I should decide on something?
- Out of those beliefs or values, which of them already help me?
- Out of those beliefs or values, which of them hurt or keep me suffering in some way?
- What people, places, or organizations (spiritual, religious, educational, political, or other) have contributed to my current belief systems around making choices?
- What did my family of origin believe regarding this idea?
- What is something I wish for regarding this idea and in relationship to how I live my life?
- Do I notice any dichotomous (all or nothing) thinking patterns regarding the idea above that keep me suffering?
- Do I notice any conditional statements I make regarding the idea above?
- Do I notice any pressures I put on myself regarding making choices or knowing what to do?

The Art of Discernment Is a Sovereign, Lifelong, and Unfolding Process

We get stressed when we can't figure something out or make a sound choice. We forget that we weren't meant to be able to discern everything by age eighteen when we turned into an adult.

Then when we are at every age thereafter (thirty, forty, fifty, sixty, etc.), we still get upset and frustrated with ourselves when we have difficulty making a choice.

We tend to shame ourselves and have internal thoughts such as, *I should be able to make this choice because of my age. Why do I struggle with making this choice? I am too old to be indecisive or unclear about things.* And there are many more. Yet we forget as time and life moves on that we have more experiences that will happen to us, shape who we are, and shift who we are in new ways. Think of it as adding more applications into a software program. Now we have a new software program and need to learn how to adjust to it. Every new piece of information adds another element to our decision-making process.

Earlier in this book, we discussed that learning and growth are fluid, lifelong experiences, the metaphor of cycles and set points in growth, and how everything is always changing. If we are thirty years old, and we have never in our life experienced a family conflict or argument, we will not know how to discern what to do in that situation. If we are sixty years old, experience our first job change, and feel ambivalence and uncertainty around the choice, how will we know how to discern what is good for us? It has nothing to do with age. We can only make choices based on the information, resources, and experiences we have had at that point in our timeline. Even though society tries to tell us that we must meet these developmental milestones at certain ages or have this certain set of life experiences at other ages, it does not mean it is true.

Because everything is fluid—time, beliefs, values, culture, desires, wants, needs, and the list goes on—it would make sense that our discernment ability is also. Thus, notice society's hidden expectation of, *I should always be able to decide on something, and if I can't, something is wrong with me.* It is incorrect. It is normal at any age or developmental stage to have ambivalence while making choices and to feel uncertain. As human beings, we are fluid. Our existence is fluid in its entirety.

The fear of making the wrong choice is just that: another fear and something totally made up in the mind. We forget that we are allowed to make choices and then change our minds five minutes, two weeks, or two years later, which go against that original choice. We have way more freedom in this than our ego or mind allows us to see.

If you start one job and do not like it two weeks later, quit. Yes, you may disappoint others in that process, yet it is better to leave something you do not like rather than stay in it. If you've been a CEO of a company for thirty years and have hated it to your very core, quit. Obviously, there are consequences to that. If you are stuck in an unhealthy and toxic relationship or family dynamic, leave. But the illusion that we don't have a choice is what keeps us stuck in pain. We absolutely have a choice, at any time, which we can make to feel freer.

Also, let people think what they want to think about and judge your experience. At the end of the day, you are the one who was brave enough to be true to who you are and what you want. Others have a hard time understanding the idea of freedom and sovereign choices because we live in a society based on control.

Change your mind, make a choice, change your mind again, and make another choice. Give yourself grace and compassion to be able to do that as many times as you need to and until it fits you. Find play during your process of the art of discernment across your life. Don't allow others to tell you that you're wrong. Fight for your right for sovereignty as a human being who is allowed to learn as you go. It's your life, and your process.

Journal Prompts

1. How many times in your life did you avoid making a choice out of fear of what others would think or of disappointing others?
2. Make a list of the decisions you have made in your life thus far that seemed scary at first but ended up being the best decisions you ever made. Notice those and ask yourself why they were the best. Is it because you felt freedom and more alignment with what you wanted or needed at that time?
3. Make a list of the decisions you have felt regret over in your life thus far. Ask yourself what you regret about those? Were your decisions based on what someone else wanted you to do or what you wanted to do at that time? Did you learn anything from the regret? Notice the lessons. Notice if you made choices based on someone else's idea of what your life should look like. Do this without judgment on yourself.

After-Reading Reflection

- Was there anything from this section that resonated with me and that I would like to start using and practicing in my life?
- Moving forward in my life, is there anything from this section I would like to slightly modify to fit my way of thinking and believing and my value system? (Remember that you are here to explore and create your own values.)
- Is there anything I read that brought up something I would like to talk to a loved one or family member about?
- Based on my values related to this topic, what are my boundaries around this regarding other people? And what will I do when someone does not respect my boundaries around this idea?
- Moving forward, how will I discern what is healthy versus not healthy for me in regard to this idea?
- Moving forward, my new relationship with the idea or philosophy is_____.

CHAPTER 6

The Fear of How We Learn from Our Relationships

Potential assumptions and fears say, *My relationships don't teach me. How do I make meaning from a connection that was hurtful? People will leave me. People who leave or hurt me are no good. I'm afraid about my own worthiness. The pain I felt from this connection wasn't helpful for my learning.* Spaciousness and flow say, *All my relationships have the capacity to teach me. I can discern if there is a lesson to be learned and what that lesson is.*

Before-Reading Reflection

- What is my current relationship like with believing that connections teach me?
- What are my current beliefs about the idea above?
- Out of those beliefs or values, which of them already help me?
- Out of those beliefs or values, which of them hurt or keep me suffering in some way?
- What people, places, or organizations (spiritual, religious, educational, political, or other) have contributed to my current belief systems?
- What did my family of origin believe regarding this idea?
- What is something I wish for regarding this idea in relation to how I live my life?
- Do I notice any dichotomous (all or nothing) thinking patterns regarding the idea above that keep me suffering?
- Do I notice any conditional statements I make regarding the idea above?
- Do I notice any pressures I put on myself regarding the idea above?

A lot of us already believe this in some way. Yet when we are upset about something going poorly in a connection, we sometimes externally blame the other person because it is easier to do so. But once we have calmed down, we are able to take the higher perspective and analyze lessons in and from those connections. Carl Jung was the pioneer in stating that relationships were mirrors and that everything that irritated us about others could be a reflection of learning for ourselves.

It is OK if you do not believe that every person comes into your life to teach you something. Yet you can still benefit from the activities in this section for self-exploration. If you do have this belief or acceptance, it helps you grieve relationships differently if they change. It also helps you have more awareness of the current dynamics of relationships in your life. It helps you drop more into neutral thinking, which helps you feel more at peace.

The following is an activity that explores if and the way you feel some relationships in your life have been teachers. Think of all connections in four different categories: reinforcers, illuminators, motivators, or shields. Reinforcers are people who come into our lives to remind us about something that is great about us and to reinforce it. Illuminators are people who come into our lives to show us, illuminate, or highlight something that could be worked on within us. Motivators are people who come into our lives to inspire us in some way. They illicit that passion within us. Shields are people who come into our lives to protect us in some way.

You can also layer these four with the labels of primary, secondary, and tertiary, in terms of levels of closeness. For example, a partner or spouse would be a primary. A best friend would be a primary. A coworker would be a secondary. A very distant friend would be a tertiary. All four categories are different variations of teachers. If you reverse that, you have served these purposes for others on your life path as well. And sometimes people may serve two or more of these purposes and vice versa. This metaphor can be used with romantic, platonic, family, and coworker connections. To be clear, I am not labeling humans' odd things here. I am using these terms to represent the energy dynamics in any connection.

Sometimes in connection, we experience the same lesson repeatedly until we learn it, whether that lesson came from a person whom you would categorize as a reinforcer, illuminator, motivator, or shield. This means that sometimes we have similar people who keep appearing in our lives to show us something. This is a two-way street, as we teach people also and play these roles in their lives. That is the mirroring effect of relationships. I think of this as our souls calling in reinforcements for a lesson we are trying to learn.

For example, dating is a teacher. Do you notice in dating and romantic connections how much your mind plays into things? For example, say you have three dates with someone, and he or she disappears. You think a variety of thoughts such as, *What an asshole. They suck anyway. It must have been me. I wasn't good enough for them*, or anything in between that spectrum of thoughts. Your ego will make up so many things. Your spirit will say, *That person came into my life experience to show me something, but what is it?*

Well, maybe that quick tertiary person you dated was just here for a blip of time to remind you how to love yourself and that you are whole without needing someone else. Maybe they were there to remind you to learn discernment in dating. Maybe they were there to share one quick moment to remember how beautiful you are. The change in perception helps process these changes and losses differently.

Sometimes dating teaches us how to love ourselves, not be offended by someone else's lack of readiness for a relationship, discern between someone's emotional availability or unavailability, respect yourself, and make self-honoring choices. That mindset can help you move on a little easier from perceived rejection. You can't blame others for their sovereign choices in love.

I think it's important to note some good old phrases here. People can only love you based on their level of emotional self-awareness, healing, and growth at the time you meet them. Nine out of ten times, they are not rejecting you; they are rejecting love because of something within them. Ask yourself, *What is the experience with this person showing me? What do I need to notice, without judgment, about myself right now? How can I reduce the intensity of my judging of this other person right now?* This applies to non-romantic and platonic connections as well. We get out of that ego-based space, which keeps us stuck in pain, and instead, we move to a more neutral space. We can be sad because of a relationship that ended or that someone didn't choose us. But to fully process that energy out of our systems, we must eventually look within.

People have personal preferences across all types and roles of connections. They are not bad or good; they just are. If you do not fit someone else's personal preferences, why would you want that person anyway? Ask yourself that. The answer is most likely related to the fear-based thoughts regarding rejection. *Because that person didn't pick me, I must not be good enough.* Change that to, *That person had personal preferences that were not aligned with mine. That is OK. I will find someone else with whom I am more aligned.*

Sometimes we must accept that not everyone we love will love us back. That does not mean that you are not worthy of love. It also doesn't mean that your love for the person wasn't real because it wasn't reciprocated. It is also OK to grieve those instances.

Now let's take this and apply it to people in our lives. This activity may take some time depending on the number of connections you want to look at in your life.

1. Name some people who fall into one or more of the categories that describe energy and connection below.

Reinforcers:

_____

_____

_____

_____

Illuminators:

_____

_____

_____

_____

Motivators:

_____

_____

_____

_____

Shields:

_____

_____

_____

_____

2. Take some time to write down the lessons each of them taught you.

_____

_____

_____

_____

3. Take some time to write down the lessons you think you may have taught them.

_____

_____

_____

_____

4. In your romantic connection(s), what role does your current partner play? What role do you play in your partner's life?

_____

_____

_____

_____

5. What roles did your parents or caregivers play in your life? What role do you currently play in their lives?

_____

_____

_____

_____

6. What role did close friends play in your life?

_____

_____

_____

_____

7. Is there anything you would like to consider about your connections in general after reading this? Is there any way you'd show, react, or respond to someone differently if you fully leaned into all connections being teachers?

_____

_____

_____

_____

I'd like to give this disclaimer: We don't allow toxic situations to stay in our lives because we have a belief that all connections are teachers and that they were meant to be in our lives. This is about using discernment. It is meant to be a guide to explore connections and not an excuse or reason to keep someone in your life who is hurting you!

8. With that said, are there any people in your life who are playing a role that doesn't fit into any of these four categories but just takes up your energy and space?

_____

_____

_____

_____

If we accept that others are teachers, we allow space for wisdom to come from all our connections, which helps us grow and become unstuck from cycles of pain.

After-Reading Reflection

- Was there anything from this section that resonated with me and that I would like to start using and practicing in my life?
- Moving forward in my life, is there anything from this section I would like to slightly modify to fit my way of thinking and believing and my value system? (Remember that you are here to explore and create your own values.)
- Is there anything from this reading that brought up something I would like to talk to a loved one or family member about?

- Based on my values related to this topic, what are my boundaries around this regarding other people? And what will I do when someone does not respect my boundaries around this idea?
- Moving forward, how will I discern what is healthy versus not healthy for me in regard to this idea?
- Moving forward, my new relationship with the idea or philosophy is_____.

CHAPTER 7

The Fear of Defining Love across Our Lives

Potential assumptions and fears say, *I am not loveable or worthy. If I love, I will get hurt. I may make the wrong choice in the person I love. I fear defining what love is across various relationships.* Spaciousness and flow say, *We are all made up of love. We get to define and redefine what love is to us in a fluid way across our lives. Love is a state of being, an emotion, a choice, and an intention.*

Before-Reading Reflection

- What is my current relationship like with the word love?
- What are my current beliefs about love?
- Out of those beliefs or values, which of them already help me?
- Out of those beliefs or values, which of them hurt me or keep me suffering in some way?
- What people, places, or organizations (spiritual, religious, educational, political, or other) have contributed to my current belief systems?
- What did my family of origin believe regarding this idea?
- What is something I wish for regarding this idea and in relationship to how I live my life?
- Do I notice any dichotomous (all or nothing) thinking patterns regarding the idea above that keep me suffering?
- Do I notice any conditional statements I make regarding the idea above?
- Do I notice any pressures I put on myself regarding the idea above?
- What fears do I have surrounding romantic love and partnerships?
- What insecurities come up for me in my relationships?
- Have I ever felt confusion about what love is and is not?
- Have I ever disconnected from a romantic relationship out of the fear that I wasn't good enough or of getting hurt?
- Have I ever felt someone else judge me for whom, what, when, or how I love?

Eckhart Tolle stated, "Love is a state of being." It is simultaneously an emotion and an intention we have internally and a choice we make and express externally. Underneath all the fear, love is what we are made up of. It is said by those who study the science of the soul that the soul is energy made up purely of love. It is one thing in life we question so much. Who do we love? Who do we want to love? Who don't we want to love? How do we love?

27

There is an ancient story from Hawaii that speaks to one way we tend to view romantic love (Gregory 2020). The Hawaiian flower called naupaka is a legend on the islands. Naupaka is the name of a beautiful Hawaiian princess. The story says that she fell in love with a man named Kaui. When they met on the beach, Kaui was working as a fisherman. As soon as they saw each other, it was love at first sight.

Kaui was considered a commoner. The two lovers were not permitted to be together since Naupaka was royalty. Even though their families did not permit them to be together, they were told that they were allowed to pray to the gods. So the couple prayed to the gods but to no avail. They were still not permitted to be together. Naupaka took a flower she had in her ear, tore it in half, and told Kaui to take half the flower and go live down by the water. She would stay in the mountains.

From there, they separated. Their half of flowers grew where they lived. The male flower by the water, and the female flower was in the mountains. The legend says that the lovers will be reunited after the flowers have each been picked from the land by the water and from up in the mountains and joined as a whole flower again—reunited.

This legend can engender inspiration and hopefulness within us. The two flowers when connected made a whole, indicating, you should not lose hope that someone out there is perfect for you. Naupaka and Kaui supposedly never ended up together. That's heartbreaking.

For the purposes of discussion around romantic love, here are a few questions for you. Do you believe in destiny, in soul mates, and that there is only one person out there for you? Or do you believe love is more of a choice you make and that you choose someone you want to spend your life and work through the hard times with? There are no wrong answers to these questions.

If you believe in one aspect, that belief can also change over time, as it is fluid. You can believe in both—that we all have soulmates and that love is a choice we make. We choose, and destiny tells and shows us.

Also, the legend talked about their love being forbidden. And in a general sense, I want to show you how that might happen in our own families. Sometimes the family of origin we come from and societal, religious, and spiritual beliefs all impact our decisions in choosing who we love.

Take a moment to reflect on the following questions. Write down your answers here. What do I believe about romantic love?

_____

_____

_____

_____

Why do I believe that?

_____

_____

_____

_____

What do my family members tend to believe about this subject?

_____

_____

_____

_____

How does that impact or not impact my decision on choosing a partner?

_____

_____

_____

_____

Notice any fear-based thoughts that come up for you surrounding romantic love. Notice any love-based thoughts that come up for you surrounding romantic love.

Now let's talk about unconditional love as a state of being. Regardless of who our romantic partners are, we are still made up of love. And therefore, whether we believe in destiny or not, we are capable of loving whomever we want to because we are made up of love itself.

Love is a state of being because we are made up of love. (Tolle 2001)

Love is an emotion because we feel love.

Love is a choice because we have sovereignty to choose love and with whom.

Love is an intention because we want to express love.

And when we remember these four aspects of love, we give our heart permission to love in the way we want to. Also as family members, we don't judge others for their choices of partners if we are able to remember these.

Since love is a state of being, when we are acting out of love, we are not judging but rather coming from a neutral, compassionate space. For example, let's say a parent does not like the person his or her child is dating or marrying. Technically, that parent could respond to this from a neutral space. They could say, "Hey,____, I just want to talk to you about my concerns

29

regarding your choice of partner. I am concerned because_____." Now, the point would be that the concerns are not expressed in terms of a judgment but more as a question. "I am concerned that _____ might not be the best fit for you because I see the patterns of interaction you two have together that are hurting each another." Say that instead of, "I think that person you chose is an asshole and just not good enough for you."

Unfortunately, the later statement is how some parents and family members express their love and concern to their children. In conscious connections and parenting, we are asking out of curiosity instead of judgment. When parents talk like this to their children, they place hidden agendas, conditional statements, or what can be perceived as conditional love. A conditional love thought says, *I have to choose a partner that my family will approve of, or I could lose my family.*

It is a hard thing for parents to accept that their children might know what is best for themselves, that they as parents do not know everything, and that they are still learning and growing across their own lifetimes. Their intention may be out of love, but it's certainly not always felt that way.

That is one example of how miscommunication can occur. All parents, kids, and grandparents should take the four statements about love above when discussing romantic love. We turn those into questions to ask ourselves before we engage in a discussion about romantic love partners. Ask yourself,

1. Before I speak to this family member, do I remember that I am made up of love and therefore capable of discussing this in a conscious way?
2. Before I speak to this family member, do I remember that the love I have for him or her is large? While yes, I just want the best for that person, am I expressing the love I have for him or her in what I am about to say?
3. Before I speak to this family member, am I remembering that we have the sovereign choice to love whom we want to?
4. Before I speak to this family member, are my words intentional in how I express my concern rather than judgmental? Is it my intention to understand and discuss? Or is it my intention to control?

Love is a state of being because we are made up of love.

Love is an emotion because we feel love.

Love is a choice because we have sovereignty to choose love and with whom.

Love is an intention because we want to express love.

The above-mentioned concerns in family dynamics are pretty commonplace in the family therapy office. It is all well intended, as family members want what is best for one another.

Yet the manner in which things are approached can be hurtful. So while this section seems to be twofold, it is all related.

To choose conscious partners, we must be aware of our own beliefs surrounding romantic love and what love is in general. To have conscious family connections, we must be aware of our own beliefs surrounding romantic love and what love is in general. But we also must learn how to have conscious discussions around a family member's partner whom we don't agree with. It doesn't matter what generation you come from; everyone has the ability to have open discussions from curious spaces rather than judgmental spaces.

Unconditional Love

The space of unconditional love is something we all desire to have access to in our lives. Yet at times, our minds forget that we already do have access to it at any given time. Unconditional love says that I love you without conditions. You don't have to work for my love. It just exists. You don't have to jump through hoops to earn my love. You don't have to do anything for it. You don't have to change yourself to receive it. You don't have to be anything. You don't have to be any version of what our minds might put on each other to define your role in our connection or family for me to love you. You can just be you, and we can grow together. I don't have judgments upon you in any way. You are just you, and I am just me, and we exist. We are malleable, fluid spiritual beings having a human experience.

Unconditional love is indestructible, as it is just there. It cannot be created or destroyed, as it is energy. It accepts you at any stage of your development and has zero judgments about your process, as it does not hold space for fears or worries. There is no earning, bartering, deal-making, compromising, sacrificing, eliminating, or leaving; it's just a frequency that is.

And we are either living within that space or sometimes temporarily stepping outside of that space when we feel fearful and worried, or we are in pain. We may leave it for a while and then go back to it and feel peace, serenity, and bliss. And sometimes this is repeated. We leave it, but it doesn't leave us. We have access to it at any time we want or need it. Our minds are what say it has left us. Our spirits know it never did. Our pain makes us feel that we aren't allowed to access it and that we are not worthy of it. We base it on things measured by the intensity of our pain. Our mind wants to make sense of the pain from the past or assumptions of the future. We step outside of the present moment or longer, depending on our level of pain and willingness to process something that has happened to us. But we always have a choice to step back into the space of unconditional love.

When something hurtful happens to us, we need moments to allow the feelings to process the energy out of them and for the feelings to flow through us. If we allow it to naturally take its course instead of resisting, controlling, and avoiding, we can jump back into that frequency. If our minds choose to take an elongated detour (to judge, blame, or shun another) by avoiding the pain and instead focusing outward on blame, as a natural by-product, you stay off that frequency longer. It's not bad; it just is.

Thus, we have a few choices we can make when we feel pain. How am I going to allow myself space to feel the feelings? How am I going to reckon with the other person or people involved, who may not be acting from a self-reflective or compassionate space that honors both feelings? How am I going to respond to the people who don't want to join me in that space? And am I as an individual willing to look at my own judgments that were and are part of these dynamics?

When I go within, I show unconditional love for myself and others. If I am willing to look within myself, it shows unconditional love for another. It says, *I love you enough to look at myself in all my weaknesses as well.* If we are willing to do that, the pain that we all feel is more temporary, and it flows away. It will not extend the cycles as long.

We all have trauma and pain underneath our stories, which are the same pains, emotions, and feelings. Unconditional love recognizes that. Regardless of our stories, our pains are very similar. We all feel fear and worry in the same way. We all feel unconditional love in the same way. The feelings are not different.

Yet in matters of the heart when we have trauma, we tend to live in the past moments of it, as well as trying to guess the future that will happen. But if we pull back to the present moment, we can find safety in that. We can find safety in unconditional love in the present moment. And, if we are able and willing to do that, it does not mean we are better than the person who cannot do that. It just means that the specific person or people are not yet able or willing to do that. Maybe the other person needs more time in a different space to deal with multiple things that they are experiencing. And in that situation, unconditional love allows the spaciousness for people to have their experiences without judgment. It says, *I respect and love you enough to not add to your difficult experience now.*

Being on the frequency of unconditional love is a sovereign choice and right that we all have access to. Sometimes it is hard for people to see this and the hope it offers because of traumas, fears, and the conditional programming of society. Yet we absolutely have the ability to create our reality in terms of love, our relationship, and our access to it at any given point on our timeline. It is fluid.

As part of unconditionally loving ourselves, though, that doesn't mean we judge ourselves for being off the frequency for a bit or for having cycles of pain that make it difficult to remain on it. We just notice it without judging ourselves and give ourselves grace and compassion.

In ancient Greece and the Bible, there are three main types of love. Eros is romantic love, philia is brotherly love, and agape is God's divine or unconditional love (Roat 2022). Yet our spirits long to feel agape or unconditional love across environments, people, and places. They long for the unconditional acceptance that agape or divine love offers us every day. Eros and philia love—the loves of our romantic connections and friendships and families—can feel fleeting at times because of the conditional statements we place on one another in our minds. Yet God's divine love, agape, is always there. It never moves. It's right there in front of us every day. We have full access to it. And we all long for agape to infuse all our connections.

Unconditional love does not equal unconditional acceptance. Unconditional love accepts that our minds are sometimes capable of making conditional statements. It says, *I accept that you are human too and have the capacity to make hurtful statements or do hurtful things.* Yet unconditional love and acceptance of how our minds operate and compassion for another's process does not mean we need to keep people in our lives. (This will be discussed later in the book in more detail.) It says, *While I accept that you are human, and I am too, in order for us to both be in peaceful spaces, we may need a break, pause, or temporary disconnection.*

Our frequency, vibes, moods, and emotions are fluid and malleable as humans because our decisions, choices, and intentions are always in flux. Yet agape is the one thing that doesn't flex. Unconditional love stays right where it is and does not fluctuate, leave, or abandon us. We must remember that we all have access to it. The same can be argued for perceived negative emotions like fear. We have access to fear, worry, and pain anytime we want it. If we want more of it, we can certainly jump on a timeline for it.

Unconditional Love is therefore a state of being, an emotion we feel, a choice because we have the sovereignty to choose love, whom we love, and when we love, and an intention because we want to express and receive love.

After-Reading Reflection

- Was there anything from this section that resonated with me and that I would like to start using and practicing in my life?
- Moving forward in my life, is there anything from this section I would like to slightly modify to fit my way of thinking and believing and my value system? (Remember that you are here to explore and create your own values.)
- Is there anything from this reading that brought up something that I would like to talk to a loved one or family member about?
- Based on my values related to this topic, what are my boundaries around this regarding other people? And what will I do when someone does not respect my boundaries around this idea?
- Moving forward, how will I discern what is healthy versus not healthy for me in regard to this idea?
- Moving forward, my new relationship with the idea or philosophy is_____.

CHAPTER 8

The Fear on Compassion

Potential assumptions and fears say, *If I have compassion for another, it somehow shows weakness. People who are different from or hurt me don't deserve my compassion.* Spaciousness and flow say, *My capacity for giving compassion to another is endless. Yet I get to discern if, how, and when I utilize it across my life span and in a fluid manner.*

Before-Reading Reflection

- What is my current relationship like with the word *compassion*?
- How do I decide who deserves my compassion?
- How do I decide how I view another person's weakness?
- What are my current beliefs about the idea above?
- Out of those beliefs or values, which of them already help me?
- Out of those beliefs or values, which of them hurt or keep me suffering in some way?
- What people, places, or organizations (spiritual, religious, educational, political, or other) have contributed to my current belief systems?
- What did my family of origin believe regarding this idea?
- What is something I wish for regarding this idea in relation to how I live my life?
- Do I notice any dichotomous (all or nothing) thinking patterns regarding the idea above that keep me suffering?
- Do I notice any conditional statements I make regarding the idea above?
- Do I notice any pressures I put on myself regarding the idea above?

If we accept others' perceived weaknesses and limitations (and our own), we are free from the chains of judgment, and we find compassion and forgiveness.

Every single one of us carries an invisible umbrella around with us all day. Sometimes it is put away and wrapped back up so that we can go to work. Sometimes at work, it pops back open. The umbrella serves as a mask for the outside world—shield or layer of protection. Sometimes it feels very heavy, and sometimes it feels light.

The storm we all go through may be different experiences and narratives, but our umbrellas and what is underneath the umbrella are similar. The storms that hit us are all different. We have gentle rain, hail, a medium-sized downpour, lightning and thunder, wind, and mist. They all carry a different level of emotion and experience.

On the top of the umbrella, there are human words that we use to label ourselves and one another, such as narcissist, borderline personality, fear of abandonment, fear of rejection, fear of worthiness, etc. Sometimes our hearts allow us to close the umbrella for a little bit. It's usually after we remember who we really are—soul, spirit, and not the mind. All of the umbrella is the mind.

When looking at someone else, I often think, *How does this person's umbrella seem? How long has this individual been carrying the umbrella? How often? Has this person ever been able to put the umbrella down or away? Does the energy with which this person currently holds the umbrella seem like it's something he or she is willing to change? What can I do or say to make this person feel safe to bring his or her umbrella down?*

If we apply this with curious minds in all our connections, we can feel more connected to others and less judgmental. The behaviors we engage in are a reflection of the label of the umbrella, shield, and storms that got us there. For example, think of someone who has self-identified as a person who experiences narcissistic tendencies. That person's umbrella had labels on it, such as narcissist, fear of making errors, fear of imperfection, fear of worthiness, fear of rejection, not good enough, or must know everything. His or her outward behaviors were guarded, shut down, isolating, telling white lies, competitive to a fault, self-righteousness, not accepting of love or help, highly judging others, rigid in behaviors, etc. All of these behaviors stem from the root of the label on the umbrella. This is a collective issue of the ego and mind.

And here is another example of someone's umbrella: a female whose labels on top say perfectionism, fear of rejection, fear of abandonment, not good enough, insecure, and unworthy. Her storm is slightly different than his is. However, their umbrellas are oddly similar, right? So here they both are—this male and female—standing with their umbrellas that are oddly similar. This is an unspoken truth. They are standing there, unable to have a conversation.

But what does the process of the umbrella being put down look like? How do we discern what feels OK and safe for us in relation to our expectations of others putting their umbrellas down? How do we discern if that means someone should stay in our lives or not? How do we discern if we should even put it down and have a conversation?

The judgment we hold against another while also holding our own umbrellas is what kills us and our connections. My dear, you are already carrying your own umbrella. And because we are, what right do we have to judge another's umbrella (story, mask, behaviors, and process of change)?

Who says someone's umbrella is misplaced or that it should have been healed by now? Who says, "You're too old for this behavior," "You're too late in your realizations or progress," or my favorite, "My umbrella sparkles more than yours does. My problems are shielded in sprinkles, and they have a different story; therefore, your umbrella is inexcusable." Who decides what any of that should look like? Some people may look at the female's story and find more empathy just because her behaviors are less outwardly expressed toward others. But males' narcissistic tendencies are more visual; therefore, he isn't in the right.

Our umbrellas are all the same. To think otherwise may be considered self-righteousness. And that self-righteousness is ironically found in behaviors that are outwardly expressed from your umbrella. Humbleness says without judgment, *You do hurtful things, and so do I. We all have our pain, and it is displayed in different ways. That does not make one person's pain of any less value or realness than the next.*

And then our umbrellas start to close because we realize that some things about ourselves and others have healed a bit. We begin to let the light in instead of holding in the darkness. When we do that, others standing with their own umbrellas always judge that process, again because of what is on their own umbrellas.

Do you believe people can change? If you don't, you will always only see that person's umbrella. Take a step back and really look at how this affects and shows up in all your connections and relationships in every domain of your life—work, family, in-laws, and anyone else. We struggle to remember this about being human.

What would it be like if for one day, the people in the collective all put their umbrellas down simultaneously? Or if they just noticed or saw that person's umbrella with more compassion? How would we react to others and the world around us? How would we move through life differently? At the same time, would there be any lessons for our souls to learn if we didn't have those umbrellas? Would it make our world incredibly boring?

The key here is to be mindful of one another's umbrellas in our interactions. Slow down and be curious. Notice how our umbrellas affect one another in connections. If we recognize what's on our own umbrellas and how they show up for us, we can be aware. If my umbrella has fear of being unworthy written on it, and yours has fear of abandonment on it, we can work with it instead of against it.

Activity: Stop, Pause, and Reflect

1. Take a moment to think about at least one person whom you had a difficult time accepting or understanding or someone you simply didn't like. Think about the worst parts of that person, which you just didn't like. You can think of one or more.

2. Now, draw your umbrella. Write the labels words and fears on the top of it. Note the storms (or stories) you have been through, which have cast those words on your umbrella.

3. Now draw the other person's umbrella. Draw what you perceive for that individual to be labeling on his or her own. Write down what you know about that person's storms (stories) and the labels you think that individual has in his or her mind. Think of labels such as unworthy, fear of failure, fear of abandonment, fear of rejection, etc.

Ask yourself, *Do I know enough about this other person's storms to have any judgment here at all?* The answer to that will vary depending on your closeness with that person. If you have never been emotionally vulnerable or intimate with that person, how would you know? We can say with 100 percent certainty that we don't know the details of another person's storm. We only have fragmented pieces of anyone's story—sometimes even with the ones we have been most intimate with.

4. Get curious about what you do not know. What don't I know about the other person's variations and the intensity of his or her storms? Do I know how this individual's parents treated him or her? Do I know the generational patterns in his or her family? Do I know his or her trauma? Do I know every word someone has said to him or her that was hurtful? Do I know every time someone else made him or her feel unsafe? Do I know every time that person was ever told or made to do the right thing and how that shamed him or her over time? What else don't I know? Notice the assumptions you made with limited information about another's experience.

5. Now write all the judgments down that you have made about that person. Don't hold back. And literally don't judge your judging right now.

_____

_____

_____

_____

Do you notice anything about those judgments? Do you notice that your judgment could be related to something on your own umbrella (your own narratives and stories)? See this as a moment of reflection in a mirror. What you saw in another's umbrella in the rain just reflected back to you in a puddle. We are energy bouncing back and forth from one to the other.

Look at that puddle's reflection instead of the person. That, my friend, is a glorious space for healing, growth, and learning. What this person did to you when you perceived it as a hurt reflected something back to you that you needed to learn about yourself or life. The magic of rainbows, spectrums, and storms is that it illuminates across time and space. And it never ends.

In the puddle between our umbrellas is that space of compassion. In that space, I see compassion, grace, understanding, forgiveness, and unity because at the end of the day, we are all love—this space of nonjudgment and neutrality.

6. Let's apply this to your life moving forward.

Does this change a value for you?

_____

_____

_____

_____

Does it make you want to see others in a new light?

_____

_____

_____

_____

Does it make you want to reconcile with anyone you know?

_____

_____

_____

_____

Does it at least make you want to hold space differently for someone in your life (even if it is someone you just have to deal with)?

_____

_____

_____

_____

7. What beliefs, thoughts, or behaviors did you already have surrounding these concepts, which have helped you in the past? What situations do you think you already do well with in terms of compassion and nonjudgment?

_____

_____

_____

_____

I'd like to add this disclaimer: I am not saying to accept others whom you truly do not want in your life. Nor am I saying to accept less than you deserve. I'm just inviting you to look at all of your connections that feel different and to free yourself from judgment. Judgment holds so much of your daily energy. On the other side of that, there is freedom.

What I project, others receive. What another projects, I receive. You choose. Choose the reflection in the puddle for your own growth. Choose to see the whole picture with compassion. If I reflect on my umbrella of love and forgiveness, it is what shows up in the puddle between us. If I reflect fears, worries, and judgments, they show up in the puddle between us and vice versa. Furthermore, just because one person's umbrella is currently bogged down, full of fears, and labeled with worries, it does not mean that your umbrella has to be also. Hold your vision.

Intimacy says, *Lower your umbrella. Let's lower them together.* Let's always be willing to look in the reflection of the puddle before blaming one another or reacting. I am willing to see my reflection first and how that affects my perceptions and reactions to you before judging your umbrella. And we need discernment on assessing how to know when it's safe to put it down. Sometimes, we need space between the puddles to allow time and the reflection to do their jobs. It's OK to take a minute or one hundred minutes to slow down.

After-Reading Reflection

- Was there anything from this section that resonated with me and that I would like to start using and practicing in my life?
- Moving forward in my life, is there anything from this section that I would like to slightly modify to fit my way of thinking and believing and my value system? (Remember that you are here to explore and create your own values.)
- Did anything from this reading bring something up that I would like to talk to a loved one or family member about?
- Based on my values related to this topic, what are my boundaries around this regarding other people? And what will I do when someone does not respect my boundaries around this idea?
- Moving forward, how will I discern what is healthy versus not healthy for me in regard to this idea?
- Moving forward, my new relationship with the idea or philosophy is_____.

CHAPTER 9

The Fear of What if I Forgive

Potential assumptions and fears say, *If I forgive, it makes me weak. If I forgive, it will allow others to hurt me again. People who have hurt me don't deserve my forgiveness.* Spaciousness and Flow say, *Our capacity to forgive is endless, yet we get to discern who, if, when, and how we forgive another across our life span. Forgiveness of another frees our minds.*

Before-Reading Reflection

- What is my current relationship with the concept of forgiveness?
- What are my current beliefs about the idea above?
- Out of those beliefs or values, which of them already help me?
- Out of those beliefs or values, which of them hurt me or keep me suffering in some way?
- What people, places, or organizations (spiritual, religious, educational, political, or other) have contributed to my current belief systems?
- What did my family of origin believe regarding this idea?
- What is something I wish for regarding this idea in relationship to how I live my life?
- Do I notice any dichotomous (all or nothing) thinking patterns regarding the idea above idea that keep me suffering?
- Do I notice any conditional statements that I make regarding the idea above?
- Do I notice any pressures I put on myself regarding the idea above?

Your forgiveness is not contingent on your growth process or level of change. You don't expect the other person to change before you forgive.

We have all been in those situations where it is extremely difficult to forgive someone, whether it is for a perceived small, medium, or large offense (a comment, a relationship of any kind ending, or mental, physical, or emotional abuse). Pain comes on a spectrum, and our willingness and readiness to forgive someone else does too.

We can't accept and forgive until we are ready to do it. It can't be forced, pushed, rushed, or controlled. Therefore, the pace at which you need to forgive is OK. The important point is that we do not judge ourselves in that process but rather allow ourselves the time and space to process the emotions.

Before moving on, ask yourself, *Who am I thinking about while reading this section? What relationships or connections have I had the most difficulty with in terms of forgiveness?* A very common thought pattern that the ego mind can get stuck in is, *If I forgive them, it means I am allowing the same thing to continue, that I am weak, that they don't deserve forgiveness, or that I will lose my power if I forgive.* In some extreme situations such as physical, emotional, or sexual abuse, it might be true.

However, forgiveness doesn't mean you are letting the person off the hook. Rather, you are freeing yourself from cycles of getting stuck in pain and victim-mindset cycles. It's saying, *Today, I choose forgiveness because the energy of this pain is becoming too overbearing for me.*

All emotions hold energy. According to HeartMath LLC, pain, resentment, and anger are "depleting emotions." And emotions such as love, peace, contentment, and forgiveness are "rejuvenating/replenishing emotions" (HeartMath 2023). Ask yourself, *What do I want to spend more time in?* If the answer is that you want to be more in love, peace, and contentment, choose a pathway that leads to forgiveness. I am sure that no one who is reading this is thinking, *Yeah, I want to stay in resentment and pain. That sounds fun.* We don't want that. Our ego wants to stay stuck.

We sometimes have a person whom we have perceived making twenty different offenses against us, which we have to learn to forgive. At first our thoughts may say, *I cannot see a future reality of me forgiving this person at all, I cannot believe this person did this to me,* or, *I don't think I will ever heal from this.*

Firstly, it is important in any connection to self-reflect on how your own history, fears, trauma, or behaviors have impacted the connection. So that is step one. Ask yourself what patterns of behavior or cycles within yourself are playing out currently in this specific connection. You will be surprised at what comes up for you. While you may not have deserved what that person did to you, you sometimes are an active participant in allowing it to keep happening.

Forgiveness is possible for almost any situation or connection. It will lead you to more grounded heart-centered living and less pain. Our capacity to forgive is endless. It literally breaks the chains of pain and sets you free. And when that happens, you begin to do it more across various situations because you see how useful it really is.

Managing our expectations of others goes a long way as well. Just because we believe in X, it does not mean the other person does. If we let go of the expectation that others should think or behave in the same way we do, we free ourselves more.

The following are examples of how to forgive others for small, medium, or large offenses what the potential growth point could be, and the reflection you could see in the situation. The format is this: You will be looking at what your ego thinks versus what your higher self says in situations. Your higher self can mean many things to many people. I am using it in a general sense here. Higher self means the voice of reason and the heart-centered, compassionate, and grounded self. This can assist us in not personalizing everything.

Example for Forgiving a Parental Figure

Ego Self

My mother is an A-hole. She constantly makes comments about body image, food, and exercise. It's like she does it on purpose to make me feel bad. I can never forgive her for hurting me so much.

Higher Self

I recognize that our parents are human too. If my mother is making comments about body image, it must mean that this is something she struggles with internally and that she is projecting it outwardly. I acknowledge that this hurts my feelings and that she is in pain. I can forgive her for being human and set boundaries as needed.

Growth-Point Considerations

I can heal my own wounds and relationship to body image. I can set boundaries of this moving forward.

Example for Forgiving a Current Spousal or Romantic Relationship

Ego Self

My spouse/partner never listens to me. When I tell my spouse/partner that I need help with chores or duties around the house, it's like he or she purposely ignores me. My spouse/partner never listens to me when I discuss any emotion at all. It's a hamster-wheel cycle, and I can't ever forgive him or her for it. There's too much history and pain.

Higher Self

I am conscious of my need to feel validated, seen, and heard. I acknowledge my feelings. I also need to try and understand what is causing this lack of presence in our connection. There may be something my spouse/partner can't or doesn't know how to say right now. I can seek clarity from him or her.

Growth-Point Considerations

Ask yourself, *Are there other areas of my life where I don't feel validated, seen, heard? I can self-reflect on this. I can also ask my spouse/partner more about his or her experience—if he or she is exhausted from something else in his or her life or if there is something I am doing in our dynamic that is contributing to this pattern in our communication.*

Example for Forgiving Ex-Spouses and Romantic Relationships

Ego Self

My marriage was ruined because of him or her! It was ruined because of that person's narcissistic behavior, manipulation, and gaslighting. It's all that individual's fault that my confidence and self-worth are completely gone. I can't forgive or move past this.

Higher Self

I recognize that even if my ex has a narcissistic personality disorder or tendencies, they are from a state of pain and masking. This means that while all of it is very painful and real, acknowledging and recognizing that my pain was a form of projection can help me heal. It may take a long time, but I can forgive at a pace I am comfortable with.

Growth-Point Considerations

I can look at my own self-worth as an individual and the way it plays out in the relationship patterns of my life. I can engage in self-love and self-acceptance practices to heal.

Example for Forgiving a Friend

Ego Self

Ugh! Every time I am with this friend, he or she always talks over and one-ups me. It's like he or she is doing it on purpose. He or she doesn't value me and our friendship.

Higher Self

There are a few possibilities as to why this person is acting this way. He or she could be trying to impress you because he or she values you. Or maybe that person is struggling internally with his or her own concept or relationship with the meaning of success. I am allowed to feel annoyed by this and to see this as a projection of something within him or her. I can ask myself if I subconsciously do it to him or her also.

Growth-Point Considerations

I can have a conversation with this friend assertively and compassionately. I can explore my own relationship with success, what it means to me, and why it is bothering me so much.

Example for Forgiving Extended Family Members (In-Laws, Aunts, Grandparents, Etc.)

Ego Self

My mother-in-law brought cheesecake to the family function when I specifically asked her not to bring anything. She never listens! She is always trying to control everything and acts like the matriarch of the family.

Higher Self

First, this isn't just about cheesecake. What I am really upset about is feeling unheard by her. Also, why does it truly matter that she brought cheesecake? It doesn't hurt anything that she did. I recognize that I am triggered because I like to feel in control. And when I feel someone else is trying to control, it's hard.

Growth-Point Considerations

What other areas of my life do I feel a lack of control in? Why is it that I feel safer when I am in control? What patterns in my upbringing or other areas of my life have had an element of control? How can I learn to let go of control more and to enhance my own well-being, become less triggered, and feel freer?

Example for Forgiving a Child

Ego Self

These damn millennials! They are so selfish with their time. My son/daughter never visits or spends time with me. It's like he or she doesn't care about me at all. All that matters is his or her self-care time, career, but not quality time with loved ones.

Higher Self

I recognize there are generational differences between us. My feelings are hurt by the situation. I can refrain from personalizing it so much. I see that their generation has its own battles like mine did. I recognize that it is not their fault. I can still talk to them about missing them and express it from a compassionate space.

Growth-Point Considerations

I can look at ways to assertively communicate with the people I love. I can tell my child that I miss him or her. I can recognize that I am mad at the societal structure of different generations and not my child. I can have meaningful dialogue about this with my child, without judgmental statements.

Example for Forgiving a Stranger, Random Person off the Street, or Someone at the Local Grocery Store

Ego Self

That jerk didn't hold the door for me! He literally let it slam right in my face while he was playing on his phone. Ugh. How rude!

Higher Self

I recognize that I cannot hold others to the standard I hold in my values surrounding politeness. If I let that expectation go, I will be freer.

Growth-Point Considerations

Review your general values list and societal belief systems. Explore how you'd want to handle it in the future when others don't live up to your values.

I hope these general examples will apply across varying connections in your lives. I truly believe this can be used for anything—even politics. Yes, I just said that. A simple higher-self statement for anything political would be, *I recognize that the person has his or her own reasons for believing the way he or she does on this specific timeline of life. I honor the fact that this individual has his or her own beliefs. There is absolutely no reason to argue about it. It will only drain my energy.* This idea and difficulty will be discussed in more detail in another chapter.

Practice using the formats in this chapter with people whom you have difficulties with in regard to forgiving. Try to find the neutral space that makes you feel grounded and more at peace. I am not saying that we always must be nice. We are allowed to feel and experience our emotions. We all have egos because we are human. It's in acceptance and forgiveness that we recover and find peace in a neutral space.

After-Reading Reflection

- Was there anything from this section that resonated with me and that I would like to start using and practicing in my life?
- Moving forward in my life, is there anything from this section that I would like to slightly modify to fit my way of thinking and believing and my value system? (Remember that you are here to explore and create your own values.)
- Is there anything I read that brought up something I would like to talk to a loved one or family member about?
- Based on my values related to this topic, what are my boundaries around this regarding other people? And what will I do when someone does not respect my boundaries around this idea?
- Moving forward, how will I discern what is healthy versus not healthy for me in regard to this idea?
- Moving forward, my new relationship with the idea or philosophy is_____.

CHAPTER 10

The Fear of Accepting Our Different Perspectives

Potential assumptions and fears say, *Two things can't exist at once. I must choose a side. I don't want to pick the wrong team. If I don't always stand 100 percent on my values or beliefs (and fight others to the death on it), I am going against my own beliefs.* Spaciousness and flow say, *Our capacity to see another's viewpoint or perspective is endless. Yet we get to choose how we interact with different perspectives. We don't have to agree with one another on everything to get along. There are technically no rights or wrongs. We are all allowed to be fluid in our perspectives in a giant, vast space.*

Before-Reading Reflection

- What is my current relationship like with the idea of two different perspectives existing at once?
- Is it difficult for me to accept that others believe or feel something different than I do? If so, in what circumstances or situations is this true?
- Do I notice any complications in my relationships regarding having a difficult time with each other's perceptions?
- Do I ever try to control another's viewpoint out of my own frustrations and beliefs?
- What are my current beliefs about the idea above?
- Out of those beliefs or values, which of them already help me?
- Out of those beliefs or values, which of them hurt me or keep me suffering in some way?
- What people, places, or organizations (spiritual, religious, educational, political, or other) have contributed to my current belief systems?
- What did my family of origin believe regarding this idea?
- What is something I wish for regarding this idea in relation to how I live my life?
- Do I notice any dichotomous (all or nothing) thinking patterns regarding the idea above that keep me suffering?
- Do I notice any conditional statements I make regarding the idea above?
- Do I notice any pressures I put on myself regarding the idea above?

If we accept that there are unlimited amounts of perception in this world and on any one topic, we can have conversations that do not involve heated arguments. Perception is subjective. It is also vast and limitless, and it takes up a lot of space between our beliefs. According to Altman and Mata, the process of perception has three main stages: selection, organization, and interpretation (Altman and Mata 2014).

The first stage is selection, which includes using our five senses with all the stimuli around us. Our human brains cannot attend or respond to all the stimuli around them at any given time. Thus, we choose what we want to pay attention to and when. This is a process called sensory selection, which helps us determine the stimulus that gets our attention. We base what we choose on salience, our needs at that time, our expectations, and our interests. Salience is described as anything that attracts our attention. An object, an idea, a quote, a concept, or a particular person can be salient. Salience is what is important to us at that time.

For example, when you are a social-media influencer, and you are scrolling on social media, and you come across content related to that subject, you will pay attention to that content and scroll past the rest if it is not important to you. We all do this. We pay attention to what is most important to us and ignore or pay less regard to what is not important to us.

The second stage is organization, which includes processing stimuli by blending external stimuli with internal processes. How we perceive the world is determined by our internal worlds. Similarity, proximity, and primary and recency effects are described here.

If we are similar, we are more likely attracted to one another. If we are not similar, we may distance ourselves from one another. We also create stereotypes in our minds, as it is easier for the human brain to do. Proximity refers to us paying attention more to what is close to us.

The primary and recency effects refer to how we see something. Primary effect refers to what we see first and tend to believe. Recency effect refers to the opposite, meaning that what we see last, we believe most. For example, there's a first impression. If we meet someone for the first time, and they smile and buy us flowers, we have already placed this person in our minds as a positive one. An example of a recency effect would be to say you had an hour-long, deep conversation with someone on many topics, but what the other person said last stuck with you most. That is now how you perceive that individual most.

The third stage in the process of perception is interpretation. Altman and Mata describe many factors that impact how we interpret our perceptions. I want to share a few of the points related to our connections with others. They discuss how our brain desires to be right. Confirmation bias is our tendency to believe evidence that supports preconceived notions while ignoring or disregarding evidence that is contrary to our desired reality. In other words, we don't see things as they really are; instead, we see things as we are.

Attributions refers to the interpretation process by which people make judgments about the causes of their own behaviors and the behaviors of others. How we interpret this has a direct correlation on our relationships and interactions. There is something called fundamental attribution error, which is the tendency to attribute others behavior to internal rather than external factors. In other words, you attribute a person's behavior to who that person is rather than external factors.

Self-serving bias is the attribution process that we engage in to portray ourselves in the most desirable light. Research shows that we do this easily with ourselves, but we do not so easily offer the same grace to others. When we are the perpetrator of an undesirable behavior, we will likely place blame on some type of external attribution (i.e. it's the other person, the time, the weather, etc.). On the contrary, when we are the victim of undesirable behavior, we place blame on the internal attributes of another (his or her character, accusation of being inconsiderate, etc.).

And finally, the last categories they discuss are the halo and horn effects. The halo effect occurs when initial, positive perceptions lead us to view later interactions as positive. The horn effect occurs when the initial negative perceptions lead us to view later interactions as negative.

All this is to say that humans are incredibly biased. It's not our fault. It is how our human brains are designed. We have a desire to believe that our reality is right. Yet all this science of psychology simply states that we are not right, and we are also not wrong. We simply see what we see—and others do too—at the time we see it. Yet every one of us misses things by default of the human brain. There is simply not enough time to tend to ideas, realities, and perceptions that our needs and interests don't desire. We only want to tend to what is important to us or what stands out to us; that is salience.

If you remember nothing else in this book, remember this chapter. Knowing how we perceive the world around us makes us humble and helps us give grace to others' perceptions when they are not the same as our own. We are just doing the best we can as we go along. And, as we perceive and interpret new stimuli and information, we integrate more of that into our system. The more aware of all of this we are, the better our connections with one another are. They are more open-minded, peaceful, and intentional.

None of us is right, and none of us is wrong. Technically, there is no such thing. There is only a whole lot of space between our perceptions and realities. Spaciousness, vastness, and limitlessness are the keys to having conscious connections with those we love because in that spaciousness, there are things we cannot see and perceive called blind spots.

And Is the Way to Love

Marsha Linehan created dialectical behavioral therapy. In her treatment model, she talks about the usefulness of the word *and* in interpersonal relationships in her workbook (2014). The word *and* is one of the most impactful and useful words. It is the most boring word to the visual and auditory senses when it's all by itself. However, when positioned between two competing ideas, it's the most beautiful adjunct that we all need in our lives.

Below are examples of and statements, followed by you making your own statements.

We can love someone dearly and know we shouldn't be with him or her.

We can dislike the freckles on our human bodies and still love and value our bodies.

We can be mad about something and still be kind and compassionate.

We can believe in Christianity and can appreciate and value other forms of faith.

We can believe in spiritualism and still appreciate and value other forms of faith.

We can truly dislike someone and still respect him or her as a human being.

We can be learning something new and be an expert on something else.

We can be going through a difficult time and still find humor in it.

I can decide today about any one thing, and tomorrow, I can change my mind on that one thing if I desire and can make a different choice.

When we as a collective use more ands, we become softer hearted and more compassionate. You don't even have to agree with me on the use of the word and. I can believe in the use of the word and, and you don't have to, and we both can move on with our lives unscathed. But if you're interested in conscious connections, I highly recommend you buy into it.

The concept of non-duality and reducing dichotomous thinking have been the main themes of this book. Duality damages our relationships and connections more than anything else. And statements help support you while trying to drop out of duality and into connection.

But where is the line of discernment between accepting other viewpoints, perceptions on things, and who that person is and letting it be? I know there are a few things in life we cannot make and statements for—rapists, child molesters of kids, and murderers. We might find empathy regarding their stories of what turned them into people who hurt other people, as their stories must be dark. However, it's hard to say things like, "I believe in world peace, and you can be a murderer." This is an extreme example though.

What are the beliefs you cannot say and for? I am not saying you must and up your entire life. Yet notice the places where it feels right intuitively for you and its usefulness. Also notice the ways it does not. What will you do with the things you cannot turn into and statements in your personal life? How will you engage, interact, and respond to these people, places, ideas, and things? Those most important questions deal with how you will use your own discernment and awareness surrounding the ands. Ask yourself what distress, anxiety, depression, or other symptoms may arise if you use ands or if you don't. What situations you use or not use ands for your relationships and boundaries.

Practicing and Statements

1. Write down all the ands you'd like to weave into your life. These can be things you typically think all or nothing about. Or these can be things that play out in your connections.

_____

_____

_____

_____

2. Look at your family, platonic, and romantic relationships. Think about the people you love dearly and get incredibly frustrated with in conversation. Start there. Replay a conversation or two you've had with these individuals. Notice how that feels somatically on your body as you replay it. Notice what parts of the conversation you could have approached differently if you allowed another person's perception to exist without a reaction. Now replay it again in the way you just imagined.

Did that feel better for you somatically than the original version did?

_____

_____

_____

_____

How would that relationship improve if you did that?

_____

_____

_____

_____

How do your mind and heart feel about that as a new version?

_____

_____

_____

_____

Do you feel lighter, more at peace, more curious, and less defensive?

_____

_____

_____

_____

If you don't feel lighter, more at peace, more curious, and less defensive, why not? What triggered you there?

_____

_____

_____

_____

When we find ourselves in ongoing arguments of any kind, it's not that we are wrong for arguing or having ideas, passions, and beliefs. They aren't bad. It's amazing to have passion, purpose, and ideas. It's just what we do with them when they are different from another's. What a different variety of connections we can have when we spend time in this spaciousness—peace with one another and internally.

After-Reading Reflection

- Was there anything from this section that resonated with me and that I would like to start using and practicing in my life?
- Moving forward in my life, is there anything from this section that I would like to slightly modify to fit my way of thinking and believing and my value system? (Remember that you are here to explore and create your own values.)
- Is there anything from this reading that brought up something I would like to talk to a loved one or family member about?
- Based on my values related to this topic, what are my boundaries around this regarding other people? And what will I do when someone does not respect my boundaries around this idea?
- Moving forward, how will I discern what is healthy versus not healthy for me in regard to this idea?
- Moving forward, my new relationship with the idea or philosophy is_____.

CHAPTER 11

The Fear of Defining Emotional Intimacy

Potential assumptions and fears say, *To be loved, I must have my shit together. To be loved, I must always feel whole. To be deserving of intimacy, I must be perfect, fixed, and healed. To love, I need to try to fix, control, and change myself or others.* Spaciousness and flow say, *Intimacy does not expect perfection; it expects growth. We do not have to be whole or 100 percent healed to be loved. We do not have to agree to have a connection; we just must understand one another. We are allowed to be fluid and evolving while also having connections with others.*

Before-Reading Reflection

- What is my current relationship with emotional intimacy?
- What are my current fears about emotional intimacy?
- How do I relate with my own insecurities or imperfections?
- How do I relate with my partner's and non-romantic connections' imperfections?
- What are my current beliefs about the idea above?
- Out of those beliefs or values, which of them already help me?
- Out of those beliefs or values, which of them hurt or keep me suffering in some way?
- What people, places, or organizations (spiritual, religious, educational, political, or other) have contributed to my current belief systems?
- What did my family of origin believe regarding this idea?
- What is something I wish for regarding this idea in relationship to how I live my life?
- Do I notice any dichotomous (all or nothing) thinking patterns regarding the idea above that keep me suffering?
- Do I notice any conditional statements I make regarding the idea above?
- Do I notice any pressures I put on myself regarding the idea above?

Have you ever thought you had to be perfect to be worthy of love or that you couldn't have flaws to be loved? Regarding your romantic partner(s) in life, have you ever thought he or she had to be perfect to be loved?

As humans, our minds naturally have hidden and unhidden expectations and desires regarding emotional intimacy with others. Often, we don't realize this consciously, and thus, we don't talk about it with our partners when entering a relationship. We just assume that they know—because they know us, they should just know.

What expectations do you tend to place on a partner? What do you think your current partner expects from you? If you don't currently have a partner, in general, what do you think a partner would expect from you? These also apply to non-romantic connections such as with friends and family members.

Examples of hidden expectations include these.

- I expect you to always understand me (even if I am not verbally stating a need or desire).
- Because you know me, you should just know when I want or need something.
- I expect you to fulfill a need that I haven't stated yet (such as helping me with a task).
- I expect you to fulfill an unmet need from my childhood (listening to me because I did not feel heard by parents, extra praise because I was not praised as a child, and others).
- I expect you to just do things because you love me.
- I expect you to never change and always remain the same.
- When I am having a hard time in life, I expect you to fix or fulfill me in some way.
- I expect you to always talk about feelings when I want to talk about them.
- I expect you to engage in physical intimacy with me X amount of times per week.
- I expect you to be perfect and always have it together during our marriage or relationship.
- I expect you to help regulate my emotions.
- I expect your physical body to always remain the same shape, etc.
- I expect you to be the one to make up with me after an argument or disagreement.

These are just a few examples. They are hidden because we do not consciously realize that we have them. Take a moment to review this list and consider the expectations you have had of your partners—past, present, and future partners—and the ones that partners have placed on you. Try not to judge yourself in this process. We all do this. Knowing what they are just brings awareness to them in a conscious way. Then it's something you and your partner could discuss.

Bonding and Nurturing versus Fixing and Controlling

Besides hidden expectations we can have in any of our relationships, we have the dynamic of bonding and nurturing versus fixing and controlling. If we want to have connections with our loved ones and partners that feel emotionally safe and fulfilling, we must shift from the mindset of fixing and controlling to bonding and nurturing.

When we are working from a space of fixing and controlling, it is based on fear. The reality is that if I fear something, I will show that in my outward expression to someone I care about.

This is something that infiltrates family lines and generations, right? If a grandparent fears change, his or her children will fear it also on some level and will display that as anxiety. Then their children could also. It is not a guarantee, but it is part of the bonds we have in family lines. If I fear, my child will most likely fear. If I nurture, my child will most likely nurture. This book's fifteen chapters are technically about bonds and relationships we have with ourselves about something, which is reflected outward in our bonds with loved ones and partners.

Relationships that have bonds based on fear include fixing and controlling. They can have qualities which include resisting, fighting, running away, isolating, distancing, withdrawing, aggressiveness, defensiveness, pain, gossip or rumors, judging, right versus wrong mentalities, engaging in lashing or bashing, holding space for more depleting emotions such as envy or jealousy, lacking empathy and compassion, hovering, disconnecting, rejecting, overcompensating, pushing away, and black-and-white thinking.

Relationships that have bonds based on a more nurturing approach can have the following qualities: lack of trying to fix or control another, allowing without judgment, allowing with compassion and grace, causing less pain, providing empathy, allowing being, holding space, honoring and validating feelings, respectfully disagreeing, sitting beside, connecting, accepting, holding, thinking in the gray, reciprocating, and providing spaciousness. There is a difference between spaciousness and disconnect. In bonds where we feel disconnected, we feel we cannot talk to one another without that string of tension that is thick between us. Both parties feel that they are holding on to the end of the string or rope tightly but that they are facing away from each other.

Allowing spaciousness means that I allow vastness between us to nurture, just like after we plant a seed and water it so that it will grow and bloom. This sort of invisible understanding between us is something we cannot see as easily as the disconnect, as spaciousness involves trust and faith in each other.

We do not have to agree to nurture. We do not have to parent from spaces of fixing and controlling to have a good connection with our children. We do not have to be in relationships that are perfect for them to be healthy. We don't have to agree to feel connected. We can find space between us to lower the tension and disconnect.

What points of tension or disconnect have you felt in any of your recent relationships or family bonds? On your end of the rope, what kept you there? Was it fear of communicating something to a loved one, fear that they would try to control, fix, or judge instead of nurture you, or fear of hurting the other person's feelings?

Relationships and bonds based on fixing and controlling have a hidden undertone of lack of trust or value in you. They feel that way, right? *If I share X with this person, he or she will just put me down in some way or say that I am broken or not good enough.*

Relationships and bonds based on nurturing have the opposite effect. They say, *I trust you and value your abilities and processes to figure out your own way.* Trust is a beautiful feeling. It breeds confidence within our connections and ourselves. When we feel valued and trusted, we thrive. When we feel a lack of being valued and trusted, we get confused or disheartened.

Notice the ways in which your bonds are tethered to others whom you love. To increase your awareness, notice both ends of the rope. And nurture the bonds of your blooms. Low expectations and high warmth foster emotional resiliency.

Read the statements below about true emotional intimacy. As you are reading them, take note of the statements that already resonate with you and the way you view emotional intimacy, ones that you would like to get better at, ones that you would like to talk about with your partner, and ones that you already do well at.

True Emotional Intimacy on Any Level of Connection Says This:

> I am willing to grow with you though all our developmental stages of life as humans (and with our children's stages also).

> And if our growth is at different times and processes, I will honor and respect that without judgment or competition.

> I am willing to accept what, at times, I may not understand. I don't have to understand it or experience it for me to have empathy for it.

> I will walk beside you when or if I do not understand.

> I will provide you with space and time when you don't even understand it yourself.

> I will accept that your individual journey of life is a sovereign experience, as is mine.

And at the same time, we have this life that we are trying to live together, which is another layer to our individual journey (and two separate journeys simultaneously occurring)

Intimacy says,

> I will respect your decisions and your needs even if I don't fully understand them (as it is not my job to figure that out for you).

> I respect your individual nature and needs even though we are deeply emotionally connected.

> I respect your journey and need space to do that.

I promise to understand that if or when you pull away from me, it is not personal every time you do it. You might be just struggling with something inside that you can't yet verbalize.

I promise not to pull away within a lens of fear, but I will have a lens of curiosity (and will not make assumptions).

I will recognize my own visceral and somatic responses within my fears. I promise to notice them within myself before I project them onto you.

Even if I don't like the amount of time you need to process something, I promise to take accountability for my own nervous system's response and regulation and not to impede that need of yours.

I also promise to communicate that I am feeling the above in a conscious and calming way.

Intimacy says, *I love and enjoy you at your best, and I have compassion for you at your worst. I can enjoy this life together and appreciate the value of our process of learning and growth together. We can externalize the problem as a pattern in our dynamics when we fight, instead of viewing each other or ourselves as the problem. I realize we will not always succeed with promises 100 percent of the time. I do not expect perfection; I expect progress.* The seat of intimacy is built stronger after imperfections, learning curves, and growth. Intimacy says, *I also promise to laugh at our failures sometimes, to help bridge our connection and not take life so seriously.*

As you were reading this, what did you notice the most?

_____

_____

_____

_____

If you found that you expect yourself or your partner to be perfect and never make errors, notice that without judgment on yourself or your partner. Just ask yourself how you can move forward from that idea. Can you let yourself and your partner off the hook regarding some of your expectations? What expectations do you have that could be slightly modified to allow space for those imperfections?

_____

_____

_____

_____

Have a discussion with your partner about it. Invite your partner to an open discussion. Use language such as, "I notice that I have been expecting something of you that you might not be aware of. I want to share that with you and discuss how to move forward." Or you can say, "I feel that you have an expectation of me that is hard to live up to. I would like to discuss and share this with you."

Avoid language that feels dichotomous (all or nothing or this or that) or too blaming. Examples of this include you always, you never, and it's your fault because. Also avoid trying to solve all the problems right away. Just work on understanding each other's feelings behind it. Notice conditional statements that you put on yourself regarding emotional intimacy, such as, "I am not worthy of love if I am not whole and perfect," or, "I can't always self-regulate emotions; therefore, I don't deserve love." Again, notice them without judgment on yourself and practice turning those into unconditionally loving statements. You can also use the above statements on intimacy as affirmations.

After-Reading Reflection

- Was there anything from this section that resonated with and that I would like to start using and practicing in my life?
- Moving forward in my life, is there anything from this section that I would like to slightly modify to fit my way of thinking and believing and my value system? (Remember that you are here to explore and create your own values.)
- Is there anything from this reading that brought up something I would like to talk to a loved one or family member about?
- Based on my values related to this topic, what are my boundaries around this regarding other people? And what will I do when someone does not respect my boundaries around this idea?
- Moving forward, how will I discern what is healthy versus not healthy for me in regard to this idea?
- Moving forward, my new relationship with the idea or philosophy is_____.

CHAPTER 12

Fears Related to Our Purpose

Potential assumptions and fears say, *I have no purpose. My life has no meaning if I am not doing something. If I am not producing or being productive by society's standards, I am lazy and failing. As an adult, I am not allowed to play. I must do something profound for it to mean something.* Spaciousness and flow say, *Our purpose in life is subjective, fluid, allowed to change across a life span. Our purpose can be to just exist, play, or be here to experience love, joy, all human emotions, or anything else our hearts desire.*

Before-Reading Reflection

- What is my current relationship like with my purpose?
- What are my current beliefs around how I view purpose?
- Out of those beliefs or values, which of them already help me?
- Out of those beliefs or values, which of them hurt or keep me suffering in some way?
- What people, places, or organizations (spiritual, religious, educational, political, or other) have contributed to my current belief systems?
- What did my family of origin believe regarding this idea?
- What is something I wish for regarding this idea in relation to how I live my life?
- Do I notice any dichotomous (all or nothing) thinking patterns regarding the idea above that keep me suffering?
- Do I notice any conditional statements I make regarding the idea above?
- Do I notice any pressures I put on myself regarding the idea above?

How many times in your life have you questioned your purpose or entire existence here? It's only natural. I think I have done this 5,026 times in my life so far (rough estimate). How many times have you shamed yourself about not having a purpose? Our ego or mind does all that judging. It starts to make conditional statements, such as, *If I don't know my purpose, I am not worthy.* What conditional statements have you developed in your mind surrounding your life's purpose?

If you ask spiritual leaders what the meaning and purpose of life is, you may get a similar response surrounding the words *love* and *joy.* The point is to experience as much of that as you can, to somehow help others, or to be a good human. If we accept that in life, our primary purpose is first and foremost to experience love and joy, we take the pressure off doing, and we can find inner peace with this.

So What Is the Actual Purpose of Our Lives?

Well, only you determine that. And your right to explore that is fluid across your life span. There's also a belief that once you find your purpose, you may never question it again. You have reached a pinnacle. Yet this is another trap of the mind saying, *One thing, and that's it.*

Is your purpose defined by the label of your career or what you do daily for a living? Is it defined by acts of kindness toward others? Is it defined as living a Christian lifestyle? Is it defined as living a Zen lifestyle? Is it something you do or something you are? Is it just being, existing in the present moment, and enjoying the small things?

What if purpose is not what you do, but rather, it's who you are? What if it's not what the human mind would label as a career? Those are just human labels to describe what you do. Are they your purpose? No, they are your passions and the things you do to experience the feelings. They themselves as stand-alone things are not you.

You are not anything that the mind labels in your dualistic thinking. You just are. And when you lean into this, you find freedom. What if, as you are right now, you are the purpose? It's not the things you do or the accomplishments that society places such a high value on. What if you, in your existence right here and now, are worthy without conditions? What if you are nothing that society labels you as? What if you don't have to do or be anything? What if God gave your soul the gift of freedom?

Yet our beautiful and busy minds continue to keep us feeling that we are in chaos and chains. But it's an illusion; we have had freedom all along. What if God gave us this much freedom because he wanted us to have sovereign experiences? What if he wanted us to experience and feel with less thinking? What if he wanted us to use our minds as tools to create logical steps for things Yet he doesn't want us to stay in there forever? What if he wanted us to experience the creation he made and not sit down and perseverate on existence and what we must do?

Do you think he will ask, "Why didn't you accomplish X, Y, Z?" (And if you didn't, you are in trouble.) Or do you think he'd ask, "Did you give yourself permission to experience, feel, and love during your time on Earth? Did you experience all my creation and the rainbow of human emotions? Did you spend time in nature, learn about love, and enjoy eating some cookies? Did you experience yourself through me?"

God gave us free will to experience life as we want to. He's not going to be mad at us because we became musicians instead of healers, CEO businesspeople instead of spiritual leaders, full-time mothers instead of teachers, or whatever the case may be. He loves us as is, unconditionally. Purpose is love and existence itself. The more we allow ourselves to experience and feel, the more Zen we feel. We don't have to do anything for his love. And if you believe differently than I do, that is OK. We all have the sovereign right to experience life and believe what we wish, at any given time on this journey of life.

Do you think there are dangers in believing or searching for a sole purpose or overall soul purpose—thinking we must accomplish something to earn love. It can keep us stuck in cycles of pain and the guilt-shame cycle of the mind. I just hope this invites you to consider stopping the pressure you put on yourself in these ways and to exist without self-judgment. Surrender patterns of the mind related to do, be, and have.

What if the answer to what my soul's purpose is, is nothing? What if it's to go play outside, watch the birds, or create experiences for yourself and those around you that bring you moments of peace or satori? What if the purpose is to lessen thinking and increase feeling or to give your poor overworked brain a break?

You are already the purpose. We are the purpose. And the ways we can experience his creation are infinite and endless. Our human mind will trick us and say otherwise. To the momma whose full-time job is to take care of her little ones, you are already in your purpose. You are experiencing love. To the father who is single and raising two children, you are already in your purpose. You are experiencing love. To the healer, helper, social worker, you are already in your purpose. You are experiencing the love of helping others. To the teenager questioning college, a career, and a purpose, you are already in your purpose. You are experiencing the love of freedom and sovereignty in your choices. To the middle-aged person who is working two jobs, raising three kids, and tending to your marriage, you are already in your purpose. You are experiencing a rainbow of human emotions.

Why? We are experiencing and feeling, as that is what our souls do. Our passions or what makes our aura tickle or light up are one aspect of God's creation for you. It's not singular. It's plural. So what other passions light up your aura, give you whole body chills, and make your heart chakra tingle? Leaning into those activities or passions will provide you with more experiences over and over—and that is the purpose. Experience them in whatever method you prefer. Create the experiences your soul wants.

However, as a general statement and from a psychological perspective, what the mind tends to grows. If we are thinking and worrying, we get more thinking and worrying. If we are experiencing and creating things that bring us rejuvenating or uplifting emotions, we get more of those. Yet that also doesn't discount the learning that occurs from any of our spectrum of emotions.

There's nothing wrong with wanting to feel purposeful in what you do. There's nothing wrong with any variety of passions you have in this life. The danger comes when your mind or ego attaches outcome to things such as the soul's purpose. For example, let's say your belief is that you are on Earth to be a famous musician. That's cool. You want to create music and experience all the feelings associated with sharing it. Let's say you end up creating an entire album that is epic, but you do not become famous from it. Then you are disappointed and may get in cycles of conditionally loving yourself or having depleting thoughts, such as, *I am not good enough.* The reality is that you highly enjoy the process and creation of the music. You enjoy the entire experience of it, and ultimately, you still feel proud of it.

This can be applied to any soul passion. There is a difference between sole purpose, soul purpose, and soul passion. I realize this writing comes from a spiritual and religious space in regard to purpose. You may not believe in a higher power, and that is OK. Yet regardless of if you do or do not, you have probably still questioned what the point of life is.

If you do not identify as spiritual or religious, what are the questions you ask yourself about this subject regularly? Journal about this if you wish. Answer this question: If I allowed my mind pattern to shift from what my soul's purpose to the experiences and feelings my soul wants to have, what would be different for me? Is it helpful or harmful for me to believe that I have one soul purpose here on Earth?

_____

_____

_____

_____

The essence of who you are is already purposeful. Remember who you are.

After-Reading Reflection

- Was there anything from this section that resonated with me and that I would like to start using and practicing in my life?
- Moving forward in my life, is there anything from this section I would like to slightly modify to fit my way of thinking and believing and my value system? (Remember that you are here to explore and create your own values.)
- Is there anything from this reading that brought up something I would like to talk to a loved one or family member about?
- Based on my values related to this topic, what are my boundaries around this regarding other people? And what will I do when someone does not respect my boundaries around this idea?
- Moving forward, how will I discern what is healthy versus not healthy for me in regard to this idea?
- Moving forward, my new relationship with the idea or philosophy is_____.

CHAPTER 13

The War of Being an Expert on One Thing and on Play, Creativity, and Free Thought

Potential assumptions and fears say, *I must choose one thing in my life and be great at that one thing. I can't do things that I love or that bring me joy. If it doesn't bring me money, it doesn't have value.* Spaciousness and flow say, *We all can be multi-passionate human beings. We all deserve playtime. We all deserve time to create and exist in free thought. We all deserve to explore what our hearts desire in our career across a life span. We are allowed to do a thing simply because it brings us joy. We are allowed to be fluid in this way.*

Before-Reading Reflection

- What is my current relationship like with the idea of being multi-passionate?
- What are my current beliefs about having to be good at one thing?
- Out of those beliefs or values, which of them already help me?
- Out of those beliefs or values, which of them hurt or keep me suffering in some way?
- What people, places, or organizations (spiritual, religious, educational, political, or other) have contributed to my current belief systems?
- What did my family of origin believe regarding this idea?
- What is something I wish for regarding this idea in relation to how I live my life?
- Do I notice any dichotomous (all or nothing) thinking patterns regarding the idea above that keep me suffering?
- Do I notice any conditional statements I make regarding the idea above?
- Do I notice any pressures I put on myself regarding the idea above?

In the last acceptance, we talked about how our purpose is love and joy. This acceptance refers to the fact that even though the last acceptance was true, we are multi-passionate human beings. Society currently makes us feel that we must choose one field of work for our entire lives, as if we are supposed to be experts in one thing for eternity. That alone has pressure. We spend a lot of time debating and questioning every aspect of work and career choices because we were told that we needed to go to college, get an education, and be that one thing. As we start to work in our fields after college or in grad school, we realize that doing the same thing for our entire lives can get boring. It feels like we need to suppress or repress everything else that is good about us and that we enjoy because our primary jobs consume us.

Even if you did or have no desire to attend college, you still have a lot of pressure to decide what to do after high school. And it's a decision that your mind gets stuck in thinking that the choice is final. It is never final; it is fluid and can always change.

We are basically told that we are not allowed to play or have passions or things that involve a certain amount of time, as we should be focused only on our main careers. And if we like to create, build, paint, make music, or be in a band, we are weird for taking time to do so. If we spend time in creative free thought, it can be perceived as weird or different from others. The word multi-passionate allows and gives us permission to explore what we always loved and wanted to be or do in other ways.

The following is an activity to allow yourself to explore your other passions or to remember them. This section is for teens through adults to do as individuals or to share together (if you'd like). Do you remember when you were five years old? What did you want to do when you grew up? What about at ages nine, ten, and eleven? What about when you were in high school?

Make a line on a piece of paper representing age 0 to the age you are now. Give yourself the time, space, and permission to explore this for a little while. Ask yourself the following questions.

- At what point on my timeline did I forbid myself to explore my heart and soul's desires?
- At what age did I stop dreaming of those desires?
- Who or what prevented me from that?
- What were the messages I received from others about work, productivity, a career, and money?
- Who influenced my decisions pertaining to work or a career?

As you look at the timeline you just created, what themes did you see?

- Did you want to be the classic hero (police officer, nurse, or doctor)? Did you want to be an engineer, a politician, a painter, a creator, a builder, a leader, change maker, or a speaker?
- What did your soul want in terms of career or work labels at each developmental stage of your life thus far?
- If you could do it all differently in a do-over, would you? If so, what would be different in your life as a result?

Now, pause. Sit there for a minute. Don't move. Don't even stand up and go change over the laundry. Stay right there. What do you notice from your timeline and answering these questions?

- Are you presently doing what your younger self wanted?
- Are you only doing one specific career or job and love it? (If so, that's great.)
- Are you doing one specific job and wishing in your heart and soul that it was something different?
- Are you wishing you did multiple things and had many passions?
- Are you happy?
- Do you feel joy in what you do for a living?
- Do you feel something is missing?

Ask yourself, what is my current definition of success? How has my definition of success changed over my lifetime? Add this to your timeline as well, noting when things shifted. At age five, was my version of success just to be happy, love, and have fun? I mean, our five-year-old selves are sometimes wiser than our forty-year-old selves. I can relate to that.

Somewhere in our lives, our current society got mixed up on what it is we are doing here. We forget that we are all spiritual beings having a human experience. We forgot that we can truly do anything we want to do or don't want to in this world. We forgot that we are multi-passionate creatures. We forgot that we all have unique spiritual gifts to offer. And if you said some of this out loud around loved ones or friends, you may have felt a few eyebrows raised and have wondered if they thought you were delusional. We have subconsciously buried some of the parts of ourselves that were meant to be out there and not buried. Somewhere along the line, we started to believe that we don't have any control over our own desires or destinies.

Now explore your spiritual gifts and talents.

- Do you have the natural gift of empathy?
- Do you feel you are a healer or helper?
- Do you have a lot of creative energy and desire for music or any of the arts?
- Do you have a strong sense of intuition?
- Do you craft, build, or develop?

This was a quick list. Yet when preparing for college or our futures, we tend to focus on talents in terms of areas we feel smart in already rather than on what would bring us joy or what we would be good at. We forget that we have natural gifts too.

Now pause and reflect again. Do you have parts of yourself that you keep suppressed every day to follow the social norms? If you are a parent now, how does all of this affect the way you currently parent? As a parent, you can feel depleted, overworked, burnt out, disconnected, hopeless, afraid, fearful, worried, anxious, and depressed, which the role of parenting can engender within you. I am not presuming to say that you do not have joy in your life. But the average parent in today's society feels very tired, at minimum. And if I had to guess, you can relate.

But HeartMath, LLC (2023) talks about management of our energy from a heart-centered space. When we spend a lot of time in fear, worry, and anxiety, we drain our energy (deplete emotions). When we experience other emotions such as joy, contentment, and love, we experience rejuvenating and replenishing emotions. This is a useful tool for any stage of development. But regularly asking ourselves where we are at helps us find more balance.

I know you have such an important role in your kids' and teens' lives. It is a most difficult role. No parent ever gets it 100 percent right. And there's currently zero parenting books that have every single answer on how to be a good parent. There are too many variables to consider within your role.

However, when it specifically comes to the question of how you parent your children or teens so that they grow up to have successful lives, here are a few tips. What messages do you give your teen or young adult about success? Often, if you really sit with that, you will see that much of what you say to them is out of fear, worry, concern, and the utmost love for your child. You worry for them and their generation. Will the world be in a better place when they are older? Will my kids have jobs that provide them enough money to sustain decent lives? Your intentions of what you say at your core come from loving them. You aren't intentionally trying to hurt them (even if they tell you so directly and in a fit of teen rage). Sometimes we accidentally say things that are fear based to children and teens. We do this out of our own fear and accidentally project it onto them.

Some of the things kids, teens, and young adults say in therapy regarding this topic are the following.

- My mom or dad is hard on me if I get a B instead of an A.
- My parents are pressuring me to go to college to be X, Y, or Z when I want to be a social media influencer, developer, or creator. I want to have my own business.
- I try to talk to my parents about my future, but they don't listen to me.
- My parents think I want the same lifestyle of nine-to-five that they do, but I don't want that. I wish they understood.
- I am afraid of disappointing my parents. I don't think I will be what I want to be because they will be upset.
- My parents compare me to what my brothers or sisters do, and I am not the same as them.

What themes do you notice? Could you relate to these statements when you were a teen? Can you relate now? Regardless of the generation, we all just want to be heard, seen, and valued by our parents, right? And you probably do an excellent job of this in so many ways.

Here are some tips:

- Parent from what your heart says, no what your mind (or ego in fear) says.

- Use both your nurturing energy and logic to support.
- Give yourself permission to explore the ideas of multi-passionate living, spiritual gifts, breaking the nine-to-five, and more. If you do that, you give your teen permission to do the same thing.

When speaking with them, remove words that have expectations, judgments, or comparisons.

A previous way of saying this might be, "So one of your passions is creating video games? There is absolutely no money in that. You won't have success in that, and it's a waste of time."

Instead, you can say, "So one of your many passions is creating video games. I admire your creativity! Let me help you explore how to embrace that more and support you in identifying steps that would be helpful to get there."

Being a multi-passionate human being means having the freedom to express who you are authentically in this world. We are not always just one thing or have profession. And having the freedom to do that will ultimately bring about more life satisfaction.

As adults, I am not saying we should all quit our careers and go do what our souls want right now. That doesn't sound super functional. But to know that option exists and always has frees the chains up a bit, doesn't it? And can we imagine a future for our children that is different from the one we live in now? I can visualize it. It's a life where we can have balance in our self-care and be more in tune with ourselves, connections, and passions. If we live recognizing our multi-passions, even if they are two-to-three different part-time jobs, it will ultimately bring us the happiness and emotional abundance that we all long for. We can escape the nine-to-five-plus workweek and have flexibility to work at the things we want to do, which are not determined as much by others. We can shift that if we wish.

If we base what we do not on money outcomes but on our soul's and heart's desires, passions, and gifts, we will naturally do what we love. Our relationship with money and fear can shift. We can shift it in small impactful ways. We can parent this generation through encouragement to live in passion and love and not fear and worry. It's one of the only things that can break the cycle.

In summary, parents, if you made it this far, way to go. You allowed yourself a few minutes of time to explore yourself and reflect as an individual and parent. Continue to give yourself permission for these moments and other self-reflective times. You deserve it. Trust your children's hearts and souls. If you listen carefully, they do speak to you. Trust them to make their own decisions, which are right for them. Teens, if you are reading this, cut your parents some slack. Everything they say is out of worry and concern for you and your future. They only want what's best for you.

I hope this activity has provided some awareness to both parents and teens about themselves and one another. I also hope you can talk about careers and passions in a different way to help you connect. Whatever you decide to do in life, remember that it does not have to be what some may consider grandiose or profound. It does not need to be seen by yourself or others as profound for it to be useful, helpful, purposeful, or intentional. That is another trap the mind can get into—a comparison trap.

I often ask myself a couple of quick questions before deciding to something. Will what I am doing make me lead an intentional or conscious heart-based life in some way? Will what I am doing come from a space of loving energy rather than from a fear-based energy? Will what I am doing help at least one person? If the answer to those questions is yes, that is enough for me. It does not have to be profound or grandiose. All passions have value.

It can also be difficult to be multi-passionate in terms of managing the beautiful energy of your heart. And determining how much energy or time you want to invest in any one thing. It is important to always discern your boundaries to prevent burnout. Ask yourself, *How will I be able to tell when I am overworking myself in some way? How will I manage my time and love for multiple things? How will I notice my burnout or end point of something? What are the physical symptoms I get when I am doing too much?*

After-Reading Reflection

- Was there anything from this section that resonated with me and that I would like to start using and practicing in my life?
- Moving forward in my life, is there anything from this section I would like to slightly modify to fit my way of thinking and believing and my value system? (Remember that you are here to explore and create your own values.)
- Is there anything from this reading that brought up something that I would like to talk to a loved one or family member about?
- Based on my values related to this topic, what are my boundaries around this regarding other people? And what will I do when someone does not respect my boundaries around this idea?
- Moving forward, how will I discern what is healthy versus not healthy for me in regard to this idea?
- Moving forward, my new relationship with the idea or philosophy is_____.

Jellyfish Flow for Creativity and Play

In the last two sections about purpose and passions, one of the goals for the reading was related to reducing rigidity in thoughts and societal belief systems to allow ourselves to play and flow. Regardless of our ages, we deserve to allow ourselves time for our version of play and creativity in our lives.

Ask yourself,

- Moving forward in my life, how do I want to allow myself to play?
- How will I allow time and space for either nothingness or my creative expression?
- What are my creative forms of expression? (Refer back to the multi-passionate beings' section for reference.)
- Do I prefer my creative flow to be expressed via an art medium such as paint, clay, building, music, or writing?
- Do I prefer my creative flow to be expressed more through physical activities such as dancing, yoga, Pilates, or something else?
- Can I allow myself to do any of these activities without attaching to an outcome? If I paint, can I allow myself to not care what the product looks like and avoid thinking, *I am wasting my time*?

Examples of Activities

- Create a playlist of ten songs that feed your soul. Dance to them like no one is watching.
- Put some music on and paint on canvas without expectation of outcome.
- Draw on a piece of paper without expectation of outcome.
- Go for a hike in the woods and notice the feelings you feel while in nature.

The options are endless when it comes to mindful, creative play. Anything that creates calmness in your body and helps you detach from life for a while is welcomed and needed. This is just a reminder page to do that.

Repeat after me, "Regardless of my developmental age or gender, I deserve a time of nothingness or creative play. I don't have to always be doing something. I am allowed to do absolutely nothing or spend my free time creating things that may not have a direct purpose in creating them. I recognize that by doing and allowing that, it helps relax my nervous system and detach me from the busyness of life. It also allows me time for my own free thoughts to be expressed. Moving forward, I want to_____." (Fill in the blank.)

CHAPTER 14

The War with Our Human Bodies and Wellness

Potential assumptions and fears say, *If my body is not perfectly fit, I am not worthy and lovable. I'm afraid that my physical body is aging. I'm afraid that my body isn't aesthetically pleasing. I'm afraid that I'm not eating well or exercising enough.* Spaciousness and flow say, *I do not have to always be perfectly healthy and fit or eat nutritious foods. I am allowed periods in my life when my physical wellness is not perfect according to society's eyes. My body is a malleable vessel, which changes over time. My body is allowed to change without another person's consent. I am allowed to be fluid in my relationship to my body across a life span.*

Before-Reading Reflection

- What is my current relationship like with my own physical body?
- What are my current beliefs about physical wellness?
- How do I allow myself to feel the discomfort if and when I do not feel good about my physical body?
- How do I judge myself if and when I do not feel good about my physical body or wellness?
- Out of those beliefs or values, which of them already help me?
- Out of those beliefs or values, which of them hurt me or keep me suffering in some way?
- What people, places, or organizations (spiritual, religious, educational, political, or other) have contributed to my current belief systems?
- What did my family of origin believe regarding physical health and wellness?
- What is something I wish for regarding this idea in relation to how I live my life?
- Do I notice any dichotomous (all or nothing) thinking patterns regarding the idea above that keep me suffering?
- Do I notice any conditional statements I make regarding the idea above?
- Do I notice any pressures I put on myself regarding the idea above?

Our human bodies are vessels for our souls. Eventually our souls leave our vessels and turn to dust. But while we are in our bodies, we are constantly impeded by body image and physical health and wellness.

In acceptance number six about the umbrella and puddles, do you remember the point of that? One of the points was that you reflect to others what our issues are and that everyone has them. We all know the hurtful statements everyone can make, consciously and even subconsciously, surrounding anything pertaining to our physical bodies—our weight, our thinness, our muscles, our thickness, what we wear, what we eat, if we eat, how much we eat, what we do for fitness, what we don't do for fitness, how much we do fitness, and how often. I barely need to explain here because we are all so inundated with these comments, such as, "You shouldn't be wearing that bathing suit; cover that up." Or we hear the opposite: "You're too skinny, put some meat on those bones."

But we must remember that our physical bodies aren't really us. They aren't what make you, you. Everything else in this book is the real you—who you are in your soul and your kindness, passions, and ability to learn and grow. If you look back on all that you journaled in the first several sections of this book and pull you apart the best pieces of you that you learned, that is you. The energy of your soul is you. Unconditional love is you. Seriously, write this in this space: The me of me is_____.

And I know what you're thinking. *Well, as true as that is, I still must live in my vessel while I am here.* Thus, I want to offer two interventions for you as an individual. Then I want to offer the way that families can have conscious conversations about physical bodies and health.

But first, note what your current thoughts are surrounding your own body and health.

- What do you dislike about your body?
- What do you already like about your body?
- What can your body currently do for you?
- What does your body currently struggle with doing for you?
- In what ways do you sometimes hide your body?
- Have you ever avoided social situations or events because you couldn't pick an outfit?

Now, here are two interventions for you. In the first one, I want you to read this little section called "If Words Didn't Exist." Then after that, there will be a set of body-neutral affirmations.

If Words Didn't Exist

Did you ever see the movie *Lucy*? (Besson 2014) In the movie, the main character talks about how words don't really exist and that they are only part of the human construct. They are made up so that we can make sense of and communicate in our world.

What if we only communicated through energy and not words? Imagine how less hurtful we would all be to each other. But with the idea that words don't exist, maybe that can give you some comfort. These hurtful words about bodies are just made up from societal constructs.

We are the only species who uses words to communicate. When you see two birds interacting outside, they are working in tandem without words. But they understand what they are here to do.

Words carry aesthetics, and our dualistic minds put things into categories of this and that or good, bad, ugly, pretty, handsome, etc. I once heard someone say, "The cockroach deserves the same kind of life as the butterfly." But if we see a cockroach, we are likely to kill it. The butterfly is admired for its aesthetic beauty.

We learn about words when we come into the world. When we are age two, we may look at the cockroach and butterfly, see two bugs, and know that they are two bugs. We know those are bugs. At age two, we don't realize one is prettier than the other is because we do not yet have someone who has impressed upon us that we should think that. Things just are. And while it is human nature to like things that are colorful, why is that? Because someone at one point said, "Oh, look, rainbows are pretty."

What if you were on a beach where everyone was naked, and you were only five years old. What would your five-year-old self think? Probably, *Oh, there's naked people here.* You wouldn't think, *Oh, look at those rolls, that cellulite, and those freckles.* They just are. They just exist. They are a forma physical form of energy, which changes as life does, as that is what the human body is—a form of energy—and energy changes form over time.

If we could all channel our inner child to remember what life was like before society showed us the harshness of words, we all would be living in more kindness and bliss. We would be free from the constraints of words themselves. Words are just words and a form of energy exchange. Words are necessary to us in our lives to function as a society. But they are literally just words and human-made things. Words are not us. We are not words.

Our energetic relationship with words includes things like someone saying, "You're fat." Your energetic and behavioral response shows a face of sadness. If someone says, "You're beautiful," your energetic and behavioral response shows a face of happiness.

The only reason we know we should do that is because we once learned that fat equals bad, and beautiful equals good. So now in terms of changing the relationship we have with our own bodies and health, we must rewire our brains' connections with much, including societal programming and our general relationship with words. Yet we must always come back to the fact that when we were children, none of this mattered. We didn't care. We wanted to play in the sand on the beach in our birthday suits. And we did so without any second-guessing. Everything that people say is a projection of their own inner belief systems, worries, and insecurities. It is not you.

Affirmations for My Body as a Vessel and Releasing Judgment from Others

Dear person who makes statements about other people's bodies,

I will no longer hold space in my physical, emotional, and spiritual body for your projections and judgments, which are based on your fears or past traumas.

I will no longer allow your societal conditioning and your limiting beliefs to affect my relationship with my body.

I will no longer allow your fear of intimacy to be projected onto me and your body-shaming tactics to affect my relationship with myself.

I will not engage and project back onto you because you attempted to hurt me out of your own pain.

I will not allow you to put me in a box or a label on me based on your ego's perception of what I should or should not be.

I will not hold space for any of that energetically.

I will look at you for a few minutes with empathy in my heart because you are stuck in your own patterns of self-hatred, confusion, and identity issues—but only for one minute and until I walk away. It is your job to heal that and not mine.

When you say she or he is too heavy or skinny or judge someone because his or her dinner plate is too full, I will say, "Don't you have anything better to talk about?" or, "Are you choosing to spend your energy today on judging my food or weight?"

When you say I shouldn't be wearing that bathing suit or outfit or that I should cover myself up, I will say again, "No." And I will reflect to you that you are the one stuck in societal conditioning and judgments.

When I do lose weight, and the comments shift to, "You are too skinny," or, "Put some meat on those bones," I will remind you that this is just the same as the above.

When you comment on my exercise habits that I am not trying hard enough, doing enough, or doing the right exercises, I will again ask you, "Why do my choices upset you and ask you to look within."

When you rate the male or female species on a scale of one to ten like society does in TikTok and various forms, I will turn around and ask you, "What are you missing within yourself that makes you feel the need to rate other humans?"

I will affirm myself and others to love the human vessel that they are in, at any shape or size on their life timeline, as the human vessel will change numerous times in one lifetime. The only thing certain in life about anything is change.

Repeat after me,

I love my human vessel. The vessel I was born into is loveable for all its shapes, sizes, freckles, stretch marks, and blemishes. I reject all judgments and words ever said to me about my physical form. I am a spiritual being having a human experience rather than only a physical being.

My worth as a being is not defined by my physical form. I have a God-given right as a spiritual being to love the wholeness of who I am and my mind, body, and soul.

I don't even want your validation when my body to you is perceived to be looking good or better than before, not even if they are positive statements, such as, "Looks like you lost weight; you look good." Even those words imply a judgment. It also gives the impression that you thought other thoughts in the past about my body. My body shouldn't even be a topic of your conversation.

There's a difference if it's a romantic partner affirming the other partner, but with anyone else, no thank you. I don't need your validation to know my worth based on what your viewpoint of what I should be aesthetically.

If you want to talk to me about health in any way, you will have to get out of your mind and fear-based conditioning and constructs and talk on a deeper level. If you want to talk about health in the sense of what brings you joy like running, hiking, etc., I am game.

Otherwise, I have a right to my human experience without feeling the energy or presence of your ego. I am allowed to be fluid in my own physical body. And so is everyone else.

I have a right to experience this world with peace, joy, and contentment and to love my body for everything it does for me. It allows me to hike a mountain, explore the earth, and play. And I don't need anyone's permission to do any of this.

So I reject your projection and reflect to you what you are not seeing within yourself. I invite you to look internally at you, instead of externally at me. Who hurt you in the past? Why do you comment on the body of others? What is it that you do not like about yourself that makes you so hyper-fixated on me? What has your relationship been like with body image? What were the messages you received surrounding what you should and shouldn't look like?

I am. I am consciousness. I am me. I just exist. I am not my human form; I am just my soul.

How to Talk about Body Image and Health

When talking about anything related to our bodies, whether it is what it looks like aesthetically, how or if we exercise, or what we eat, the most important aspect is removing any language that sounds like it's from a space of judgment or shaming. Examples of the language to avoid include, "It looks like you gained weight. Haven't you been exercising?" or, "What have you been eating? You need to eat better. Put some meat on those bones."

Now the next question is should we even be talking about this with someone we care about? Will saying anything, even if you have a worry or medical concern help that person? This section refers in general to how in society, we make accidental statements that are very harmful to others.

However, discerning if you should say something to a loved one out of worry for his or her medical needs is a different story. Of course, if someone has an eating disorder because of his or her concerns related to body image, we want to be a support and advocate for that individual to get professional help. Thus, we can talk about that in a gentle way, such as, "I am worried about you because I noticed _____. I am here for you and support you. I would like to assist you in obtaining a therapist."

However, when it comes to determining in general if you should comment on someone's body, nutrition, or exercise, it's a bit harder. It's natural for humans to talk about these topics, as it is part of our lives. I recommend that you ask yourself before you make a statement, *What is my goal or intention in making this statement?* If it is out of worry, use nonjudgmental and compassionate language. Yet also notice what is making you want to say something. If your desire to say something comes from a space related to your own view of what a human body should look like, and this person is making you uncomfortable because of what he or she looks like, the best course of action is to say nothing at all. Instead, go within and recognize that it's something you can modify regarding your own relationship with body and health. Words are damaging. Even one phrase said to someone about his or her body and health can stay with that person for years.

In summary, our right to our human body being fluid across our lifetime is something everyone deserves, without commentary from another. We are all allowed to have different seasons of our body's wellness across a lifetime. We don't always have to eat and exercise perfectly or rush our bodies to make changes. You deserve rest from all of those fears and ideas.

After-Reading Reflection

- Was there anything from this section that resonated with me and that I would like to start using and practicing in my life?
- Moving forward in my life, is there anything from this section I would like to slightly modify to fit my way of thinking and believing and my value system? (Remember that you are here to explore and create your own values.)
- Is there anything from this reading that brought up something that I would like to talk to a loved one or family member about?
- Based on my values related to this topic, what are my boundaries around this regarding other people? And what will I do when someone does not respect my boundaries around this idea?
- Moving forward, how will I discern what is healthy versus not healthy for me in regard to this idea?
- Moving forward, my new relationship with the idea or philosophy is_____.

CHAPTER 15

The War with Our Control and Attaching to Outcome

Potential assumptions and fears say, *If I loosen my grip, I won't succeed. If I can't see an outcome, it must not be worth doing something. I am not allowed to question my faith or beliefs.* Spaciousness and flow say, *I do not have to attach to an outcome. I do not have to grip so tightly to a result of something I do. I am allowed to flow. I can trust whatever higher power I believe in to guide me. Letting go of the need to know an outcome frees my soul to flow. I can be fluid in my beliefs, trust, and faith throughout my life span so that they can evolve and become stronger.*

Before-Reading Reflection

- What is my current relationship like with the idea of _____ above?
- What are my current beliefs about the idea above?
- Out of those beliefs or values, which of them already help me?
- Out of those beliefs or values, which of them hurt or keep me suffering in some way?
- What people, places, or organizations (spiritual, religious, educational, political, or other) have contributed to my current belief systems?
- What did my family of origin believe regarding this idea?
- What is something I wish for regarding this idea in relation to how I live my life?
- Do I notice any dichotomous (all or nothing) thinking patterns regarding the idea above that keep me suffering?
- Do I notice any conditional statements I make regarding the idea above?
- Do I notice any pressures I put on myself regarding the idea above?

Letting go of control and the need to know an outcome of something frees our souls to glow and flow like the jellyfish. Yet getting there isn't linear. It's not like we wake up one day and think, *OK, today is the day. This day and all days moving forward I will release control of all things.* I bet we all have tried that a few hundred times. It doesn't tend to work that way.

Reflect back on an earlier place in this book. The process of change and growth is a forever thing. It's letting go of control over and over and across many situations and circumstances in your life—everything we do, really. You accept that you never have control over people and most things.

Think of all the people, things, ideas, projects, work, and anything else that you have held onto regarding a certain outcome. Here are some examples: an outcome of a romantic relationship— whether you would end up together, an outcome of a conversation with a family member or loved one—hoping it will go a certain way, and an outcome of a work endeavor or project—wanting it to end up a very specific way. We grip tightly what the process or outcome of something should look like based on our minds' perceptions. If it doesn't go that way, our reactions to it are frustrating, disappointing, or heartbreaking. So in essence, we break our own hearts this way.

There is magic in the surprise of not knowing. There is magic in not being able to see what is coming, what's next, or exactly how a situation will play out. Here is a specific example. Say you are dating someone new, and you have a history of anxious attachment. So while dating this person, your thoughts start to run wild because of fears—will that person like you, stay, etc. It distracts you so much from the present moment of what is. But what's right in front of you may be beautiful just how it is right here and right now. If you allow yourself to flow out of fear, the result may surprise you. Maybe you tried so hard not to lose that person that he or she left because of that sense of control he or she felt.

Here is a second example. Say you are working on a project that you enjoy. Your mind creates organizational steps to complete the project. Your mind is great like that. It also sets the goals on specific timelines and estimates how long it will take to do something. You may make your target date for completion on October 15. By then, this will be wrapped up in a nice little bow. But does it truly work out exactly the way your mind planned it to be? Think about that. It probably never does. You are not a machine. Your mind is magical because it can make you feel that you are capable of being a machine. But you are not.

We are humans who get tired, fatigued, burnt out, and sick. We have children we care for, cars that break down, and all the life circumstances that interject themselves into that timeline or outcome. And your mind's attempt to control by staying in the timeline or outcome of that creates what? A whole lot of stress. Here's a gentle reminder to those who have gotten through every single time things did not work according to plan. In that way, you have never failed. You have lived.

Yet if we use our minds as organizational tools and also accept that they will never 100% look like we thought they would, it equals less stress. We learn to lean into flow more. But even that will never be perfect. We will never be fully in flow as we are human. It's more leaning into flow over and over again and across all situations in our lives.

Thus, instead of allowing rigidity in thought patterns to be the guide here, we allow our hearts and our intuitions to guide us. Trusting our intuitions, ourselves, and our hearts is part of flow and the inner knowing that you have and that you feel. They are all the inner voices that lead you in the ways that feel right for you, even if the mind can't fully understand it. What intuition feels like is just that—an inner knowing that something feels right for you without the mind being able to logically understand it yet.

Stripping away layers of our fears feels so good on our energetic bodies. It's a massive release. Our fears are teachers. If we don't judge our fears, just notice them, and are curious about them, it is also part of the process of flow. When you get frustrated, you cry and energetically release that fear over and over again.

For example, there is the fear of what other people think. That fear is hefty, and it runs deep. But every time you follow your intuition toward something that brings you or others joy and love, you release another layer of that fear and level up. Then you do another thing that you would normally be fearful about, and another layer sheds. You do this over and over until your true authenticity shows.

Next, trust and surrender are other large parts of flow. What does the phrase trust and surrender mean to you based on any religious or spiritual belief systems you currently have? Out of those, what belief systems and values are helpful and useful to you already? Are there any belief systems surrounding this that cause you pain, stress, or anxiety?

Trusting yourself, your own intuition, and God and the divine is what can be interpreted as trust and surrender to some. These two big beliefs teach you over an entire lifetime. If you follow your heart, it leads you closer to God. If you follow your intuition, you are following your inner guidance system. If you follow faith in God, you feel indestructible and protected.

There is a big *and* statement here. You trust God and the divine to lead you. You trust yourself to be led to God by trusting and surrendering. Trust God's plan for your life and your own ability to respond to his plan and to adapt when necessary.

Some believe that God leads us through our intuition and hearts and that is how he communicates with us. Depending on your beliefs or background this may be a triggering statement for you. What do you believe? It's OK to believe something completely different.

One of the hardest aspects of writing this book was this section, as there is a crossover between mental health and religion or spiritual beliefs of what trust and surrender mean to different people. We often choose how we trust based on our spiritual or religious beliefs. Yet it is one of the key points and most difficult things to discuss in our connections. Because of this, it can make conscious connections difficult. Thus, this may be the more difficult section of this book for folks just because of the time we are living in today, with beliefs in Christianity, Buddhism, spiritualism, and many more.

Spiritualism is defined as the science of the soul. Religion is defined as an organized structure of beliefs and values that people choose to live by. One is not better than the other, and both are allowed to simultaneously exist, just like anything else. The difficulty here is making sure that we remember what those definitions are and accept that so that we can have fulfilling relationships with one another. We inadvertently have to accept that we don't have to have the same belief system in order for us to connect. Yet some beliefs and religions may not allow or permit this ideal.

I will give a few examples here only for the purposes of clarity and not judgment. I don't what my belief system to affect yours; I just want to help others learn to discuss them and not have families breaking up.

> Christianity says that if you don't do X, Y, and Z, you will not go to heaven but instead go to hell.

Spiritualism says that there is no hell; there are just dimensions of space.

This right here has been breaking up families for decades. The difference is not one or the other! The pattern of the difference is the problem and not a system of beliefs. This is one major difference that has disconnected us from the dinner table. They are hidden topics that are so difficult to discuss because we are all so passionate about what we believe in. Passion is a marvelous thing. But learning to accept others' beliefs and passions as their own is a difficult pill to swallow at times.

Thus, conscious connections beg for and desire it. In order to have conscious connections, we must allow space for others' beliefs to exist. As individuals, we can trust, surrender, and flow in any way that our unique soul wants to. It's a sovereign choice. But to connect with one another, it requires making an active choice to accept others' differences in this way or at least accept what we cannot change.

Reflect on the spiritual, religious beliefs that impact your relationships and how you react and respond to them. Notice them without judgment. I think this book has had this undertone through it: the acceptance of all others as teachers. All beliefs are subjective.

Here are some questions to consider.

1. What are your own core spiritual beliefs that are deal-breakers in your connections (ones that you know you can't waiver on and that could inevitably cause a split in a connection)?
2. What are some of the beliefs I hold that I am OK if other people do not believe so that we can keep a connection?
3. What are the beliefs I hold that I can't understand why other people don't also believe?
4. What are my own beliefs surrounding the science of spiritualism?
5. What are my own beliefs surrounding religion and Christianity?

6. Where is the crossover or blending point of your beliefs with another? What are the common grounds?
7. Am I willing to allow space for a discussion in the commonalities of our beliefs (to see the positives in one another and build upon them)?
8. Am I willing to see the beauty in another person's sovereign beliefs?
9. Am I willing to look at the person in front of me in his or her entire journey as a human being, see that story, and not try to change it?
10. Am I willing to get curious instead of judgmental?

And if you are not able or ready to accept this part of having a conscious connection, that is OK. This is just conscious awareness of where you are at right now. That's all this book has been about. *If I am aware of where I am, that's great. If I am aware of where someone else is, that's also great. If we can connect and talk about these matters, that's great. If we aren't there yet, it is also OK. It's not necessarily good or bad; it's just where things are now.* We just don't have to agree on everything all the time for one another's values or opinions to matter.

Here is something else to notice. In any belief system we have, what makes our faith in that system stronger is proof of it over time. This means that our faith in anything gets stronger over time by the experiences we have or do not have in regard to it.

If you believe in God in terms of Christian principles, you may see his work in your life and others over time. That allows for the reinforcement of your faith. If you lean more toward the science of spiritualism and believe in intuition and tapping into your higher self to connect with the divine, when you meditate and have reinforcing experiences in that meditation in your physical life, your faith becomes stronger in that idea. And during either pathway or in any other forms of religion and faith, it is also a fluid learning process.

All of that is to say just consider it. Consider that regardless of the method of someone's religion or spirituality, it is his or her path. On any side of that, if we try to push another into believing what we believe, forcing and controlling, it will not support sustainability in a relationship. It will break it apart or provide distance.

Allow yourself to modify your beliefs. Create and play with words, concepts, and values over a lifetime. It's fun, it keeps you learning, and it is a building process. You don't have to have or know all the answers to anything at all to live a fulfilling life. It gives constant opportunities for rebirth and renewing fresh energy into your life. Glow and flow like the jellyfish. Allow others to have their processes. There is magic in the process of an individual's discernment of what trust and faith mean to him or her. Here is a nice reminder affirmation to take with you regarding the process of trusting without attaching to an outcome.

Notice, Feel, Release, Trust, Surrender, Flow, and Repeat

I notice without judgment.

I allow myself to feel the feeling.

I release it.

I trust the process and divine.

I surrender to the process and divine.

I flow in my creativity and love.

I repeat the process as necessary across life and situations—forever.

After-Reading Reflection

- Was there anything from this section that resonated with me and that I would like to start using and practicing in my life?
- Moving forward in my life, is there anything from this section I would like to slightly modify to fit my way of thinking and believing and my value system? (Remember that you are here to explore and create your own values.)
- Is there anything from this reading that brought up something I would like to talk to a loved one or family member about?
- Based on my values related to this topic, what are my boundaries around this regarding other people? And what will I do when someone does not respect my boundaries around this idea?
- Moving forward, how will I discern what is healthy versus not healthy for me in regard to this idea?
- Moving forward, my new relationship with the idea or philosophy is_____.

A DISCLAIMER TO UNCONDITIONAL LOVE IN FAMILY DYNAMICS

A Discernment that Hurts

What we do if we cannot get along is a painful hidden truth. Here is a special note for peacemakers, empaths, and people pleasers. If you have ever self-identified in your mind as a peacemaker, empath, or people pleaser, this section is for you. Do you remember how earlier in the book, we talked about the stories we all create in our minds about who we are? Well, this section may hurt for a second, but it is well intended.

In family dynamics, everyone plays a role. No one player is at more fault than another. The problem is the problem and not the individual people playing it. In any game, we know there are rules that we follow and various players. All players impact the game, right? Well, the peacemakers, empaths, and people pleasers do too.

However, there is a very big shadow side to identifying with these labels. I am sorry that this may hurt, but it is a growing pain and a lesson; I promise. If our minds identify as one of these three labels, we can accidentally and subconsciously put ourselves in a victim-state mentality. That is because we are empathetic, caring peacemakers. We feel we are somehow not at fault or part of the dynamic in a connection or family dynamic because we tried to do things to keep the peace or help. We feel that because our actions were well intended, we should get a free pass, so to speak. With that said, not everyone who identifies as one of these labels falls into these traps. Some people who identify as peacemakers, empaths, or people pleasers can discern where boundaries lie in situations and pull back.

However, in the dynamics of a family or connection, the issue is that if you are an empath, and you keep trying to help, you have become part of the family dynamic itself. You have also put yourself in a position to perpetuate the pattern. It is not your fault. You most likely did this as a survival method to be part of a family that has generational patterns related to difficulties in self-regulation and expression of feelings in safe and supported ways. That is the root cause.

Another aspect to being the peacemaker or empath in a family dynamic is that you may also be a secret holder or a keeper of the secrets that family members talk about behind closed doors.

If you were raised in a family where you were not safe to express your feelings, you were in a family that held a lot of secrets from one another. Why? Because each family member needed to vent and get stuff out since he or she couldn't talk directly to different individuals in the family due to not feeling safe to do so.

And irony of all of this is that sometimes, if you have a family of five-to-six people in a therapy office, all five-to-six people self-identified as the peacemaker in the family or the one who tried to help and fix things. This doesn't always happen, but our ego or mind again creates narratives around our self-identified labels. Now, all the people in that crowded room are on the defense because they believe they have tried to help. We must pull back from this a bit and again notice patterns and not self-identified labels in families if we want things to change. We have to remember the sameness in our stories, as mentioned earlier in the book.

Yet it is our job to notice it. Don't judge yourself for it. Notice the pattern and the way you have been part of it. You can't change the past or anything you did. Yet you can make different choices now to change the pattern or dynamic. It is not bad to identify with being an empath. But being an empath is just an identity of the mind. It can be argued that technically, everyone can tap into his or her empathy if that person is made up of love. Then we are all empaths. Maybe being an empath just means that you are aware that you have empathy and that others have empathy too. And that it is a matter of how much awareness people have uncovered about themselves in their journeys at this time. It's just that sometimes we make assumptions about another's level of empathy, which can damage relationships.

Just because you are an empath, it doesn't mean that you relate to any of the above or that by helping in your specific family you are perpetuating a dynamic. It is just something to consider. The intentions are always pure to help. It just doesn't always help. Sometimes the best thing to do is not be a player in the game. This is specific to family dynamics that include patterns related to not feeling safe to express emotions. Your family may not be at that detrimental level.

In general, though, just take a look at your role within the family dynamics. Ask yourself, *In what ways are my words or actions helping? In what ways are they perpetuating a problem in the family? Am I giving a free pass to someone I love who is constantly hurting me or another member of the family?* One way you can measure this is by how safe it is to express emotions in the family. Here are some examples.

Level 1

I cannot ever express my feelings about any topic ever. No topic is safe to discuss my feelings about. For example, if I talk to that family member or person about my feelings, he or she doesn't listen or blames it all on me. Or if I talk about my career, love life, kids, etc., there are constant undertones of judgment.

Level 2

I can express my feelings sometimes, depending on the topic. For example, I can talk to my family about feelings surrounding my career in a safe and nonjudgmental way. However, if I talk about my feelings directly to that person about something he or she said that hurt my feelings, that person cannot validate or hear me out. The other person has a hard time taking ownership of his or her part.

Level 3

I can express my feelings 70–80 percent of the time and feel safe with this family member. The little bit of resistance that person has is just over a few topics we can't talk about because of different beliefs. That is OK (a different political belief or generational belief that doesn't cause fights).

The goal is to be at level 3. That is what we all want regardless of age, generation, or developmental phase. Level 3 is in the range of the healthy expectation of a best-case scenario in any family. Some families are already at that 70–80 percent range. We can never expect 100 percent of the time to feel 100 percent emotionally safe while talking to anyone. I don't mean we should lower our expectations. We should think of what is humanly possible or not. That 20–30 percent simply accounts for general human error, such as the person having a bad day, going through a rough patch, and being stressed or acceptance of some topics that aren't good to discuss. Allow a little grace for the person in front of you being human. The problem can be that we expect too much out of humans. Consider that also.

Level 2 is that workable level. We will call it the grow zone. We have some decent abilities to make one another feel safe as we talk in our families. Yet we could use some support or assistance in ironing out some things to get better. If we can talk about these things, it shows skills in the family that could be enhanced further or tuned up.

Unfortunately, level 1 means that there is not a lot of room for growth. At this point, we need a professional's help to try and unravel the family dynamics if we want to move forward. Or we need to all sit back and self-reflect. Unfortunately, level 1 may be a good indicator that other family members in the system are not open to self-growth or learning.

The pain can be excruciating for all members involved in any family. Yet the willingness to open up and be self-reflective or not is a sovereign choice. At times, we grip tighter and tighter in family lines with level 3 tendencies. We hope that over time that things can change or that each of us will change in the ways needed to work better as a family. Sometimes we think if we just give them unconditional love long enough, they will come around. We can unfortunately wait forever and in the interim, have our feelings be completely bypassed for years and decades. No one deserves that.

Some people are just not willing to meet you in the space of compassion, nonjudgment, neutrality, forgiveness, and grace. They aren't yet ready or able to have a reciprocal conversation based on honoring one another's expressions of feelings and rights to do so. Thus, if you decide to end that connection, exit gracefully. If you want to tell off a family member on your way out, it is your sovereign right to do so and to express your feelings. Yet we can say things in a more balanced way, which is reviewed in the next section.

A Note about Humor and Discernment

In this book, we have looked at some variations in the way to have conscious conversations with family members. However, sometimes it is important to remember that "this shit doesn't always work." This is one of my favorite quotes from one of my mentors and supervisors. He was referring to therapy in general. However, it applies here as well. Because people are so complex as individuals and multifaceted, sometimes we literally can't get anywhere close to the same timeline. If you remember from chapter 2 in regard to sometimes, we jump timelines—that is what I mean. Apply that same idea here.

Sometimes due to an individual's small, medium, and large traumas in life paired with generational, spiritual, religious differences and familial upbringing and other factors, that person may simply not be interested in having conscious conversations because from that individual's viewpoint, he or she cannot see the value or need to do so. You need to accept that not everyone will jump on board here, and that is OK. Let them. Don't try to control or change it.

From there, with any connection, you have a few options. My two clinical recommendations are

1) Allow yourself to laugh at some of this

2) Discern your new boundaries within that connection specifically.

We have all been in situations where we leave family functions and say, "What the hell just happened there." Going back to the routes earlier in this book about ego or mind and dichotomous thinking, I think it is important to laugh at how our dichotomous thoughts can sometimes take over. It's no different applying it to family connections.

My own way of deflecting my own ego and humor is the following. I like to see the potential in others and these conscious connections. As I mentioned earlier in the book, I am a pretty big fan of rainbows. I want to believe because I see potential and want people to go through that rainbow portal with me. But not everyone wants to join in that. And that is OK. That doesn't mean I am righter because my rainbow portals are pretty and full of nonjudgment. But rather, it means we are just different in terms of how we perceive the world, and that is OK!

It's easy to get into a trap of self-righteousness if you strive hard to have awareness of yourself, desire conscious connections and conversations, and want to live in a space of nonjudgments, right? However, in that, we can literally start to judge others who are judging. Thus, you are now also judging. And all of it comes from the ego or mind. Then you must go back to not judging your judging. Geesh! That's a lot of that-there judging word.

This is literally the shadow side, so to speak, of conscious connections. We also must be careful not to judge others who do not believe in this or want to join us in this. Let people be who they are, on the timeline they are on, and without trying to change them. It's a freeing experience. But seriously, we should laugh at our egos. We are all imperfect.

And if we find that someone cannot join us in this, we go to discernment of what our new boundaries will be. We do not ever have to keep people in our lives just because they are family. It is OK to discern for ourselves if this is an appropriate decision for where things are at in our connections at any moment. It's ironic that this book's main intention was to do the opposite and to illuminate possibilities for change in family dynamics. Yet I would be doing a disservice to all of this if I didn't also say this.

Conscious awareness and conscious connections do not imply that you must always do the right thing. Instead, they imply that you should be aware of yourself, what you want, and what feels right for your heart.

After we learn and become aware that unconditional love exists, we also soon learn that unconditional love includes not accepting less than unconditional love from others. It is OK to yell, swear, and tell people no. It is OK to tell people off. That is not bad.

Some questions you may want to ask yourself for discerning boundaries in connecting with the family member that you don't feel aligned with are the following:

- Is this connection causing me distress on a regular basis?
- Is this connection going so far beyond my values that it causes me pain to remain in it?
- Is this connection feeling abusive to me emotionally, physically, spiritually, or in some other way?
- Is this connection continuously draining my energy more than providing me with rejuvenating energy?
- Are the issues in this connection causing a domino effect within my life and affecting my ability to focus on work, immediate family, partner, overall stress, and relationship with my other family members—child, parent, etc.?

If the answer to these is yes, you can give yourself permission to explore whether to end the connection all together or to take a break, pause, or time-out. Remember, not every decision we make must be final. We can change our minds about anything on any day of the week. We are allowed to change our minds.

Would it make sense to at least take a break from this connection for now to gain clarity and think? If so, have that conversation with your loved one. State to him or her, "At this time, I need a break or pause in our relationship. I am feeling overwhelmed by our differences. And rather than making an immediate or final choice, I need some space and time away from this to gain clarity."

When and if you take this break or pause, there are a few questions to prepare yourself for.

- In this process, how will I give myself the grace, time, and space I need to think about this?
- If a family member reaches out during this pause and attempts to poke at me in a passive-aggressive way, how will I respond? (Will I ignore that person completely or respond with a consistent phrase?)
- On the days when I start to feel guilty because I do love that person, and it's natural to feel that way, how will I self-sooth and allow myself to feel those feelings? How will I affirm and remind myself that this was needed at this time?
- What boundaries will I set in this situation during this pause and break?
- Who am I going to talk to and confide in if I am upset about this and need someone to talk to?
- How will I allow myself the space and time to reassess any or all of this during that break period?

If you discern and decide that you want to end a relationship or connection for good, that is OK as well. What you say in that situation is not as relevant or even if you say anything. However, if you want to say something, you could say, "At this time, I do not desire to continue to connect with you, and I am ending contact with you." You don't particularly owe anyone an explanation either. If you want to, you can explain further. "We are not connecting anymore in this because it is impacting my health."

A reconciliation door can be left open for those who are willing to have a reciprocated and balanced connection. Don't close your heart completely because of the pain. Just ask yourself the questions within this chapter at various points on that timeline, as your thoughts and feelings change over time in a fluid way. That is OK too. I hope this section gave you permission to laugh at and end things as needed.

CONCLUSION

I hope you have learned a bit about yourself and your connections, and your relationships through the process of this workbook. I hope you learned about yourself through exploring the fifteen internal wars and points of fluidity and peace and by discerning what feels right for you. I hope that you can apply the skills you learned in this book with family members and loved ones to build more consciously aware connections across generations. This entire book has been about love in one way or another—how we value and make self-loving choices around love, connection, purpose, careers, and the physical body and love each other in our connections.

Our Human Right to Fluidity (Flow)

I have all these rights. You have all these rights. We have all these rights. Our human right to fluidity and flow is constantly disrupted, redirected, and repressed by our society. It is the very fabric and essence of what causes our anxiety. It's the push and pull of what our hearts and spirits want versus the push and pull of society's structure and belief systems. Life will mirror this back to us all, every single day. It is the voice inside of you whispering, *Something doesn't feel right about my life, Something just feels off*, or *Is it normal to feel so stressed all the time?* That is your soul, intuition, and consciousness screaming, *This isn't right*. It's your inner knowing that life isn't meant to be this way.

In all the rushing, producing, rigid and fear-based thoughts, and questioning, we yearn to just be, flow, have inner and outer peace, and find resolution, reconciliation, and bliss. Our mind believes we must follow the rigid rules of society, and that if we don't, we are the problem. It is all an illusion.

We absolutely have sovereignty in our choices, processes, and lives. If we remember this basic human right to sovereignty and specifically, to be a fluid human being, we become free. We wear a veil of fear around us daily. This is due to the fact that we cannot slow down to allow ourselves to relax because of society's structures.

I want you to read the affirmations ahead. I want you to them repeatedly and until you buy into and allow them. Start to question. Start allowing yourself space and time to slowly adjust, consider, and assess. Ask yourself what the real problem is. I will assure you, if you've done the exercises in this book and sat in thought, you will see that you are not the problem, nor were you ever. In fact, were any of us really the problem? Was any one person or generation?

It is the belief around us thinking we are the problem that keeps us stuck. It causes us to question, *Am I doing life right?* As if there is one precise way to live a life and one way set by our society and not us. We, as individuals, did not build this society we live in now (us common folk or the non-top 1 percent. Instead, we were born into this time of chaos in our world. We sit wondering why we feel so stressed and why we can't get on the same page as our loved ones. But we have no part in the development of defining what work is. We need to produce, do, rush, and know.

But we question our entire lives in all these ways as we are walking through it. We are all alike in the ways mentioned in the book, regardless of generation or developmental milestones. This is what gets us to being One Gen. It is a simple answer.

If I am willing and brave enough to look within myself and at my own fears and to take those fears and transmute them into fluidity and love—I myself am free. If I become freer, I illuminate that possibility for others like a game of illumination tag. If I live my authentic truth, others will be inspired to follow. They will feel permission to follow. And if they do not follow, they weren't meant to. They are simply living their own sovereign life experience.

You have the power to create the life you want. It's not an easy, fast, or immediate process. It is a process that takes patience, time, and space. If you allow this for yourself, your relationships will improve as a natural by-product like the flowers in a meadow growing from the seeds next to them. You release control and rigidity. You focus on bonding and nurturing instead of fixing and controlling—as it is within, so it is without; as above, so below.

Repeat after Me

Fluid Rights

- I have a right to view all my choices as being experiences and not failures. There are no mistakes but only opportunities for learning.
- I have a right to stay in my timeline rather than jumping back over to another's timeline for the sake of keeping someone in my life.
- I have a right to treat my life as an ongoing work of art.
- I have the right to change my mind.
- I have a right to grow and change how and when I want to.
- I have a right to change the relationship I have with my own thoughts, beliefs, and values over a lifetime.
- I have the right to fluidity—to be in flux throughout my life.
- I have a right to exist without commentary or judgment from others.
- I have a right to relationships that are balanced and reciprocated regardless of the type of connection it comes from.

- I have the right to have seasons of growth and development and to take as long as I need to get through those seasons.
- I have a right to relax and to be what others would perceive as lazy. I have a right to just be and not do.
- I have a right to take the time and space I need for anything in this life.
- I have a right to process any grief, loss, or adjustment at the rate that feels comfortable for me.
- I have a right to meaningful connections, which are based on bonding and nurturing instead of fixing and controlling.
- I have a right to eliminate *should* statements out of my vocabulary as they only place unneeded pressures on me.
- I have a right to have darkness, shadows, imperfections, and weaknesses without judgment from myself. Rather, I just notice them.
- I have a right to not be perfect by what society's standards say and to define my own definition of what feels aligned and right for me.
- I have a right to my beliefs, spiritually, politically, culturally, and to allow myself to grow, expand, clarify, connect, and strengthen my beliefs over this lifetime.
- I have a right to not always do the right or just thing.
- I have a right to my human experience of what or who I was born as (religiously, culturally, and in other ways) and to learn as I grow, age, and develop, without being shunned for that experience or told that I must change that right now.
- I have the right to have connections that make me feel emotionally and physically safe, validated, seen, and heard.
- I have the right to have a healthy mindset and relationship with my human body or vessel throughout the fluctuations of change.
- I have a right to have my compassion and to discern if I give it and whom I give it to.
- I have a right to discern whom or if I forgive.
- I have a right to play no matter what age I am. I have a right to carve time out in my life for that play.
- I have a right to define what purpose means to me and to change this as I see fit in a fluid way across my life.
- I have a right to explore, create, and engage in my multi passions.
- I have a right to emotional, physical, and spiritual safety.
- I have a right to set boundaries at any given point in my life and to constantly discern and reassess this process as I go.
- I have a right to walk away from things, people, and places that are no longer supportive of my well-being.
- I have a right to take breaks from things, people, and places that are no longer supportive of my well-being.
- I have a right to assert, honor, and feel my feelings. I have a right to be in connections that honor one other in this way.

- I have a right to not feel my heart is hardened or to be bitter by the judgments I have held regarding others. I have a right to release those judgments.
- I have a right to define and redefine what love is to me across my life span.
- I have a right to trust my own intuition over any of society's structures or belief systems.
- I have a right to release control and outcomes and just be.

I have all these rights, and everyone else on this planet does too. I also have the right to do these things without judgment or commentary from others, and everyone else does too.

The irony is that some of this might sound self-centered and not out of love. But the exact opposite is true. If I make loving choices for myself, in that process, I am also making loving choices for others. While setting boundaries is meant for you as an individual, a natural by-product is that sometimes the other person on the end of that boundary learns from you. It may be painful for that individual, and he or she may not learn, but that person's sovereign choice is to make meaning of that boundary in his or her life or not to.

We all feel we have been judged, misunderstood, unseen, invalidated, and unheard. But the irony is that it is exactly what makes us the same, currently in our society. We have the same pain, even though the stories are never the same. It is in us thinking that we are different because of our pain that causes us just that—more pain. Or we measure our pain and compare it to another's. We just have to be willing and brave enough to see parts of ourselves that we don't always like in order to see another's story, viewpoint, or pain.

We can honor the feelings behind one another's stories and honor one another's stories and differences. We tend to try and relate to others who only have similar stories to ours. That itself is isolating, and it puts us in boxes. Look for the themes in the stories. We can relate and have empathy for others even if we didn't have the exact same experience.

That which lurks in our shadows and in the dynamics of our connections can be brought to light. And sometimes that light is so bright that other people are not ready to see it. That is OK. Let them go. Let them make sovereign choices and be fluid within their own lives.

We are not separate. We are the same. We are One Gen. We are a cohort of humans on this beautiful planet in chaotic times. We are just trying to do the best we can in some of the most tumultuous lives, structures, and systems. Honor that for you. Honor that for others. Allow your heart to be fluid. Allow other people's hearts to be fluid. As it is within, so it is without. Be the jellyfish. Flow, glow, and bloom together.

PART 2
Family Flow

The family flow part is for application of what was discussed in this book. The handouts are examples of the language to use with one another when talking about the subjects within the book. They are not an all-inclusive list of wording but are examples. With that said, if you decide to work on this together as a family and find extreme difficulty with it, make an appointment with a licensed family therapist for additional support.

FAMILY PRESENCE IN THE MOMENT

As we transition from looking at the fifteen areas within ourselves into the family flow section, there is an important aspect to consider in our bonds. In the journal questions within each section, there were questions asking, "What do I or my family already do well together in regard to this idea?" I want to draw attention back to that.

As humans, we are so busy that we often subconsciously forget to slow down to celebrate, adore, and admire one another for who we really are. We walk around in busy fight-or-flight mode and miss opportunities for connection. John Gottman talks about bids for connection and that we can miss opportunities for these bids in our interactions with our partners or loved ones. A bid is an attempt to get attention, affection, affirmation, or any other form of positive connection. He discusses how we turn away instead of turning toward (Gottman 2023).

We are so focused on getting through our workday, running children to activities, and being and doing all the things, we forget to live in the present moment. When we are more present and still, it is in that space that we are able to feel gratitude. It is the sweet spot of our lives. It's the spot that all of our hearts desire to stay in longer. It is painfully difficult to try to stay in that space. We are constantly sliding in and out of it.

We all have those little moments of gratitude and love until the next task of life sucks us out of it like a vacuum cleaner. Then that moment is gone. And we keep wanting to go back to that moment to the point that it feels like we resent that we can't. It's almost as if we resent our lives. In family and couple dynamics, I see this anger, sadness, and frustration because of constantly being pulled away from the present moment with one another. At the heart of that, we are mad at life, the chaos, and the busyness of our lives and not one another. However, it manifests in our dynamics as being mad at one another. We get angry at one another for missing opportunities to connect.

We then take it out on those we love. What we really want to say to one another is how bad this sucks. It sucks that we get pulled away from one another to do our chaotic schedules and routines, which we have to keep organized. What we really want to say is, "Hey, I miss you. I love you. And I am mad, sad, and upset that I can't slow down to share more of those moments with you or that we can't slow down."

I have seen couples break down after having this ah-ha moment or epiphany in therapy, in which they realize the arguments they were having were simply because they missed each other and that life just got too chaotic with children. What they really miss is having more stillness and presence with each other or having moments when they were able to show each other admiration or adoration. They miss the days when they had time to tend to and give each other a little TLC.

All of a sudden, it's not about the dishes that aren't done, the laundry, the errands, the bills, the schedules, and activities, but it's, "I don't honestly care about any of that. I just freaking miss you. I miss just being present with you."

This can be applied not only to our romantic partners but also to our children, parents, grandparents, and those close to us. What we are bad at as humans is blaming one another for this: "It's your fault you work too much. You don't do X," instead of just calling a spade a spade and saying, "I wish life wasn't so busy." Thus, slowing down to focus on being present in the moment is pivotal. In the present moment, we can show that gratitude, appreciation, admiration, and adoration to one another.

Ask yourself things such as, *This week, did I slow down to tell my partner at least one thing I appreciate, adore, and admire about him or her? Did I slow down to tell my kids that? Did I slow down to tell myself that? Did I check on my parents or grandparents this week or tell them something I appreciated or had gratitude for? We may not have this gratitude weekly, yet am I slowing down for the sake of my own sanity and the ones I love?*

I guarantee that if you as an individual slow down and find these moments of stillness and gratitude, it will be reflected outward in your connections with those whom you love. Those moments will be reciprocated over time. It may not be an immediate change, as we are talking about patterns of behavior across generational lines for decades. But this is the key to breaking those generational patterns and curses. Be who you are and express yourself from your heart space, and others will follow suit. If I flow, you flow. If I glow, you glow.

Over time, there will be differences. We just must have realistic expectations of what the process of change really looks like. It is slow. Yet notice the tiny changes over time. Have gratitude for another's effort in his or her desire and motivation for change. We can't speak of something we want another to change one time and expect it to change. We can only expect a gradual, nonlinear, and imperfect process of change.

For now, meet in the space of the present moment and stillness. Don't meet in a space of fixing and controlling but in gratitude and presence. Watch how that shifts slowly over time and creates the love and relationships you want with one another.

Thus, before proceeding further into the family flow activities, ask yourself, *How do I show the person I am reading this book for gratitude, admiration, and adoration?* If you are unsure or do not do that, do not harshly judge yourself for it. Just notice and acknowledge it. Utilize the questions within this section to get in touch with one another through compassion and nonjudgment.

A Contract between Us as Family Members

A Conscious Agreement between Us

In our connection as loved ones, I promise to do these things.

I promise to check myself first before I make assumptions.

I promise to allow space for our differences to exist, regarding values and belief systems. I promise to be curious about them.

I promise to allow you space and understanding to change.

I promise to allow you to do things in your time frame and pacing.

I promise to allow you to learn and grow and not to try to control that process.

I promise to allow you to make your own sovereign choices in matters of love, purpose, and career.

I promise not to blame you for the generation you are from or currently growing up in, as it is not your fault.

I promise that even if I don't understand you fully, I will respect your journey as a sovereign being.

I promise to remember that my words are often tainted from my own fears and worries and that it is not your fault.

I promise to be mindful of my own relationship with my body and health so as not to project my fears onto you.

I promise to try and be in a space of compassion and nonjudgment as much as my ego will allow it and at any given time (as this is not about perfection but is about progress).

I promise to see that we love one another underneath all the fears, beliefs, and values. Above all, that is most important.

I promise to try to see the underlying core belief you have that is causing us difficulty in talking about a thing.

I promise not to try to control you out of my own fear.

I promise to have grace and understanding regarding your developmental phase in life. I promise to remember what it's like to be a child, a teen, an emerging adult, and a midlife adult.

And if I am a younger person reading this book, I promise to imagine what it is like to be older and to have compassion for the generation you grew up in.

I promise to hold space for you when we are imperfect at doing any of this.

Questions and Language to Use When Discussing Book Material and Concepts

Family Flow Questions

While thinking about the content from acceptances, discuss some of the questions below. Feel free to add others as you think of them; these are just examples. The following set of questions are for exploring concerns in your connection.

- Have I ever made you feel rushed to decide about something?
- Have I ever made you feel like my own fears about change or time pressured you in some way?
- Have I ever made you feel you weren't allowed to change in any way?
- Have I ever made you feel bad about a belief you had around romantic love?
- Have I ever made you feel like I couldn't forgive you after something happened between us?
- Have I ever made you feel I was judging you harshly?
- Have I ever made you feel I assumed something about you?
- Have I ever made you feel like you couldn't talk to me about something?
- Have I ever made you feel like I judged you based on a decision you made regarding romantic love?
- Have I ever pressured you into doing a career path you didn't want to do?
- Did you ever choose a career path or go to college out of fear of disappointing me?
- Did I ever make you feel judged because of one or more of your hobbies or passions?
- Did I ever make you feel bad about your financial income or money situation in any way?
- Have I ever made you feel bad about your physical body or health choices in any way?
- Have I ever used hurtful language surrounding what you eat, how you dress, or if you exercise?
- Have I ever made you feel that I placed unfair and unrealistic expectations on you in some way?

- Is there anything from the fifteen sections of this book that stood out to you as a topic to discuss further together because you feel it affects our connection in some way?
- Have I ever made you feel that a value or belief system you have was not of value?
- What currently feels difficult for you when we try to talk to one another?
- Have I ever made you feel judged based on the generation you were born in?

If the answer is yes to some of these,

1. Talk about it without arguing regarding details. For example, don't argue if, when, or where it happened.
2. Acknowledge each other's feelings. For example, say, "I hear and understand you are upset about this."
3. Don't try to fix it right away. Just validate it and listen. For example, don't problem solve yet.
4. Give a meaningful apology to each other. For example, say, "I am sorry that when it happened, I did not recognize it at the time. I am sorry I made you feel misunderstood, unseen, and unheard in this way." Then pause.
5. Name what you will do next time something similar happens. For example, say, "Next time, I will slow down, not assume, and listen."

HANDOUT 3

Language to Use When Discussing Generational Differences in Families

Generational-Based Questions for Family Flow

The following questions are meant to be completed together so that you can converse about generational differences.

- What was an aspect of growing up in your generation that was hard for you? Why was it hard?
- How did you get through those difficulties?
- What were some of your favorite aspects of growing up in your generation? Why were they your favorite?
- What is one (or more) thing that is difficult for you when you look at my generation? Help me understand why that is difficult for you.
- Do you feel the hardships of your generation taint your view of my generation in some way? For example, what triggers you?
- What do you envy or admire about my generation?
- Is there a generation you wish you could have grown up in?
- My generation's values are_____, and your generation's are _____. If they are opposite from each other, how can we learn to accept that and interact with each another? What can we do or say that sounds compassionate and nonjudgmental?
- For example, let's say your generation's values are work and productivity and mine are self-care and wellness. When we are talking, can we be more mindful of how our core beliefs and values show up in our language around work and productivity and self-care and wellness on both sides? Can we try to modify our language a bit to lower the temperature of our conversation? Can we choose to see that none of this is any of our faults and stop blaming one another?
- Considering the core beliefs of different generations, what else do we notice that causes difficulty or tension in our connection? Is there a hidden tension that we don't discuss?
- What do we already do well in our generational differences?
- How can we learn from instead of judge each other for our generational differences?

- What is something from my generation you wish you believed or had?
- How did some of these core beliefs from each of our generations positively impact our connection? Where is the crossover lesson? How did our generations teach each other? For example, you might say, "Because you are a boomer, you raised me on the belief of hard work, so I learned the value of being dedicated to my work." The other person might then say, "And because you are a millennial, and you believe more in balance and wellness, you taught me I was working too much. We taught each other."

HANDOUT 4

Language We Use to Help Explore Strengths that We Already Have in Our Families

Family Flow Strength Based Questions

While looking at concerns is important, we also want to look at the strengths of our connections and the things we already do well together. This section is meant to reflect upon our wins and strengths.

Here are some questions to help explore what we already do well together:

- In regard to the four main categories of the book, what do we feel we already communicate well about?
  Change and time:
  Love and connections:
  Purpose and careers:
  Body and health:

- What are some specific wins we have in our past about talking about these topics?
- Why were they wins?
- What did you and I do to make the conversation feel successful for each one of us?
- What do we already appreciate about each other regarding the way we communicate?
- Do we like the way we forgive and reconcile after a difficulty? If so, what works?
- What are words and phrases I use that you appreciate or have used in the past?
- What are the positive ways we already encourage one another?
- In what ways do you feel I do not judge you?
- What is something we feel proud of one another for in our lives?
- What is something we admire about one another?
- What is something we respect about one another?
- What is something we think is interesting about the other members' generations?
- What is something we admire about the other members' generations?

Based on what we learned by doing the above questions, what will we promise to continue to do that we already know is working? (Handwrite your response below.)

HANDOUT 5

Discerning What to Do as an Individual in Difficult Topics to Discuss as a Family

Should I Say Something?

Example Scenario

The entire family is over at Grandma's house. While there, the family starts discussing the latest world, political, or human rights related news or events. The family members all start to state their opinions on the matters. In this example, let's say it's gender-neutral bathrooms. Uncle Johnny states, "This is ridiculous! Everyone just needs to remain a boy or girl and not have shared bathrooms." Let's say you believe in gender neutral bathrooms and feel his statement was highly insensitive. Before deciding whether or not to say something, follow these steps.

Step 1

First, remember the content in this book related to neutral thinking, understanding other perspectives, and using *and* statements. Notice your own judging first. Notice your somatic and nervous systems' responses to Uncle Johnny's statements. Notice that you are judging another person's judging. Ask yourself, *Is this situation a mirror to me? Have I used and statements in my mind before I say anything else to him?*

Step 2

Question your own intention or goal. Ask yourself, *By me saying something, am I hoping to change Uncle Johnny's belief? Do I wish that he would just be more open-minded because of my belief about being open-minded? Do I wish he would just stop making what I perceive to be insensitive comments in front of my children, who are also here? Do I just want him to understand how I feel when he makes these comments? Do I ultimately want our family to be able to discuss topics like this without the high intensity of emotions being present?*

Step 3

Identify your choices. There are three typical choices in these scenarios.

1. We ignore the conversation completely and say nothing.
2. We challenge it in a reactive way.
3. We get curious about it and check for clarity and understanding in a conscious way.

Yet there are consequences for each choice. If you say nothing, that is OK too. The consequence of you holding your feelings in could be that you feel you will explode later. If that is the case, choose option three to get curious and invite a conscious conversation. Yet if you choose three, it requires you to also be open-minded.

If you choose option two—to challenge it in a reactive way—it never ends well. Thus, don't choose number two. But if you cannot resist and lash out at the family member, it may temporarily feel good to you, but it offers zero long-lasting, sustainable results for maintaining conscious connections.

Step 4

Attempt the conversation. If you do choose number three, refer to the getting curious section of this book and the other *Family Flow* activity pages and invite that conversation with Uncle Johnny.

- If the conversation goes well, you can at least get to the point of mutual understanding.
- If the conversation does not go well, you learn that you cannot talk about this with that family member and discern your new boundaries for yourself in regard to these scenarios moving forward.

Discerning Together What to Do in Difficult Family Topics to Discuss

How We Discuss Together

Special Consideration Questions for Family Flow

This section of questions is for current highly triggering topics such as political values, LGBTQA+ values, woman's rights, current world affairs, finances and money, student loans, and others. This section really requires applying what you learned in the book thus far and coming from a space of neutrality and nonjudgment. The goal here is not to fix the differences in our values but to learn to understand why we have those values and to accept them.

Step 1

Choose a topic that is typically hard for you as a family to discuss.

Step 2

Before starting to discuss the topic, take a mindful moment to bring awareness to your own values, biases, and trigger points with the topic. Ask yourself, *Am I willing to put those aside for the sake of having a conversation?*

Step 3

Ask each other open-ended questions for understanding. Share your own values. Seek to listen and not to respond.

- What value do you have surrounding this topic that you would like me to know or understand?
- Are willing to share anything that has happened and has shaped this value? (It's optional for them to answer this.)

- Are we willing to accept that there is value in both of our beliefs and to use *and* statements here?
- An example is this: A person from the boomer generation believes in antiabortion rights. A person from the millennial generation believes in women's rights.
- Look at the values underneath both beliefs that are useful and compassionate.
- The person who believes in antiabortion rights values the lives of babies. The person who believes in woman's rights values women's health. Both are compassionate and both deserve space in this world.
- Can we both see the dichotomous thoughts we have about this topic (all or nothing, this or that, or right or wrong)?

Step 4

Externalize the problem. The problem is the problem and not you or me. The problem is not that we disagree. The problem is that we are both humans using dichotomous thinking. The problem is the way society operates in a mostly dichotomous, political climate. Can we agree on this?

Step 5

Uncover a potential, hidden, underlying issue in your family' dynamics of communication.

- If we are trying so hard to get the other person to believe what we believe or argue our beliefs, a hidden, underlying issue could be that we've never felt heard or understood by the others and in other situations besides this. Maybe one of you has not felt like your opinions about things in life have had value.
- If this is the case, we should stop talking about the special considerations and topics and move back into some discussions around this relational dynamic from the previous sections.

If not, proceed to step 6.

Step 6

Establish your plan.

- How can we move forward with this difference in our beliefs?
- Are we willing to accept the differences within each of us?
- Are we willing to use *and* statements to see the value in one another's beliefs?
- If not, are we willing to accept that we should just agree to disagree and not talk about that specific subject at this time in our connection?
- Are we willing to recognize that we are human, that we have the desire to be heard and understood, and that this is what causes us to struggle at times?

- How will we indicate to one another when we are overwhelmed by the topic?
- As individuals, how will we recognize when we are starting to get overwhelmed by the topic and need a break from discussing it?
- Do we promise to continue to use the conscious agreement between us from earlier in this chapter when interacting about this?

REFERENCES

Altman, Hilary, and Alex Mata. 2024. "Basic Components of the Perception Process." LibreTexts Social Sciences. https://socialsci.libretexts.org/Bookshelves/Communication/Interpersonal_Communication/Interpersonal_Communication%3A_Context_and_Connection_(ASCCC_OERI)/03%3A_Perception_and_Communication/3.02%3A_Perception_Process_-_Part_I_(Selection_and_Organization).

American Psychological Association. 2014. "Understanding Developmental Psychology." APA. org.https://www.apa.org/education-career/guide/subfields/developmental.

Besson, Luc. *Lucy*. 2014. Universal Pictures and EuropaCorp.

Bioexpedition. "Jellyfish Blooms." Bioexpedition.com https://www.bioexpedition.com/jellyfish-blooms.

Menchell, Ivan, and Clare Sera. 2014. *Blended*. Warner Bros. Pictures.

Brittle, Zach. 2021. "Turn Towards Instead of Away." The Gottman Institute. https://www.gottman.com/blog/turn-toward-instead-of-away/.

CNBC. 2023. "World Religion Day 2023: History and Significance." CNBC TV18, https://www.cnbctv18.com/world/world-religion-day-2023-history-and-significance-15661981.htm#:~:text=There%20are%20nearly%204%2C000%20recognised,Christianity%2C%20Judaism%2C%20and%20Islam.

Cziksentmihalyi, Mihaly. 1990. "Flow: The Psychology of Optimal Experience." Research Gate. https://www.researchgate.net/publication/224927532_Flow_The_Psychology_of_Optimal_Experience.

Dictionary.com. 2020. "Dopamine vs. Serotonin: The Difference between These Happy Hormones." https://www.dictionary.com/e/dopamine-oxytocin-serotonin-endorphins/#:~:text=Meet%20the%20family%3A%20dopamine%2C%20oxytocin,emotionally%20and%20trust%20each%20other.

Dion, Celine. 2017"How Does a Moment Last Forever." Beauty and the Beast. Walt Disney. https://www.disneyclips.com/lyrics/how-does-a-moment-last-forever.html.

Gill, Navdeep Kaur. 2021. "Energy in Motion: Understanding and Embodying Our Emotions as Self-Care through Ancestral Medicine." Issue of Visions Journal. Here to Help.bc https://www.heretohelp.bc.ca/visions/responding-to-feelings-vol16/energy-in-motion.

Gregory, Dennis. 2020. "The Legend of Napauka." Homey Hawaii. https://www.homeyhawaii.com/blog/legends/legend-of-naupaka/.

HeartMath, LLC. 2023. "The Science of HeartMath." HeartMath.com https://www.heartmath.com/science.

Hrla, Josh. 2016. "You Can't See It, But Humans Actually Glow with Our Own Form of Bioluminescence." Science Alert. https://www.sciencealert.com/you-can-t-see-it-but-humans-actually-glow-in-visible-light.

Linehan, Marsha. 2014. *DBT Skill Training Handouts and Worksheets*. Second Addition. New York: The Guilford Press.

Merriam-Webster Dictionary. 2024. "Transmute." https://www.merriam-webster.com/dictionary/transmute.

Merriam-Webster Dictionary. 2024. "Alchemy." https://www.merriam-webster.com/dictionary/alchemy.

Merriam-Webster Dictionary. 2024. "Consciousness." https://www.merriam-webster.com/dictionary/consciousness.

Merriam-Webster Dictionary. 2024. "Soul." https://www.merriam-webster.com/dictionary/soul.

National Center for Cultural Competence, Georgetown University. 2023. "Definitions and Discussion of Spirituality and Religion." Georgetown.edu. https://nccc.georgetown.edu/body-mind-spirit/definitions-spirituality-religion.php.

National Geographic, 1996–2003. "Bioluminescence." Education.nationalgeographic.org https://education.nationalgeographic.org/resource/bioluminescence/.

Roat, Alyssa. 2022. "What Does Agape Love Really Mean in the Bible?" Christianity.com. https://www.christianity.com/wiki/christian-terms/what-does-agape-love-really-mean-in-the-bible.html.

Rudolph, Rauvola, Costunza, Zacher, 2020. "Generations and Generational Differences: Debunking Myths in Organizational Science and Practice and Paving New Paths Forward." National Library of Medicine. https://www.ncbi.nlm.nih.gov/pmc/articles/PMC7471586/.

Shepard, Jess. 2022. "Rising Higher Meditation." Youtube. https://www.youtube.com/@RisingHigherMeditation.

Solar Schools. 2023. "Radiant Energy." Solar Schools.net https://www.solarschools.net/knowledge-bank/energy/types/radiant#:~:text=than%20long%20ones.-,Radiant%20

energy%20is%20the%20energy%20of%20electromagnetic%20waves.,Earth%20and%20
radiates%20light%20energy.

Statistica. 2023. "Resident Population in the United States in 2022, By Generation." Statistica.
com https://www.statista.com/statistics/797321/us-population-by-generation/.

Tolle. Eckhart. 2001. *The Power of Now: A Guide to Spiritual Enlightenment.* India: Yogi Impressions LLP.

Printed in the United States
by Baker & Taylor Publisher Services